Communications
in Computer and Information Science 1348

More information about this series at http://www.springer.com/series/7899

Imen Jemili · Mohamed Mosbah (Eds.)

Distributed Computing for Emerging Smart Networks

Second International Workshop, DiCES-N 2020
Bizerte, Tunisia, December 18, 2020
Proceedings

 Springer

Editors
Imen Jemili
University of Carthage
Zarzouna Bizerte, Tunisia

Mohamed Mosbah
Bordeaux INP
France Talence, France

ISSN 1865-0929 ISSN 1865-0937 (electronic)
Communications in Computer and Information Science
ISBN 978-3-030-65809-0 ISBN 978-3-030-65810-6 (eBook)
https://doi.org/10.1007/978-3-030-65810-6

This Springer imprint is published by the registered company Springer Nature Switzerland AG
The registered company address is: Gewerbestrasse 11, 6330 Cham, Switzerland

Preface

This volume contains the proceedings of the Second Workshop in Distributed Computing for Emerging Smart Networks (DiCES-N 2020). The workshop was held on December 18, 2020 virtually in order to ensure the safety of participants due to the COVID-19 pandemic. We received a total of 17 submissions, of which 8 were accepted for publication. The acceptance rate was therefore approximately 47%. Reviewing was single-blind, where each paper was assigned to at least 3 reviewers, and on the average 2,6 per Program Committee member.

Nowadays, several methods and approaches of Distributed Computing are exploited in software and hardware to propose new approaches able to support and analyze the huge amount of collected information and to deal with the control of emerging networks. Thus, the workshop tackled issues relative to the design, development, and evaluation of distributed systems, platforms, and architectures for cyber-physical systems in the context of smart cities. The program included three sessions. Session 1 dealt with Intelligent Transportation Systems (ITS), as one of the main fields investigated in the context of smart cities. ITS aim to provide users with innovative services related to different modes of transport and traffic management, in order to achieve traffic efficiency by minimizing traffic problems, such as traffic congestion, air pollution, traffic incidents, etc. The use of transport networks in a safer, better coordinated, and more intelligent way is required to offer a seamless transportation experience to road users, supplying them with useful information related to traffic, environment, and local convenience real-time running information. Session 2 focused on Emerging Networking Technologies. In fact, a smart environment involves many wide-scale cyber-physical systems, distributed platforms, and shared infrastructures, which are interconnected through a heterogeneous communication platform. Such a complex ecosystem faces several challenges such as scalability, heterogeneity, interoperability, security, and privacy. Over the past few years, several networking and communication technology innovations have emerged as a widely recognized trend, such as Software Defined Networks or Content-Centric Networks, and are extensively used to tackle such issues. Session 3 was related to Artificial Intelligence and Internet of Things. Gathering data from the physical environment relies on a huge number of real-world physical entities, endowed with sensing, computation and communication capabilities, and to some extent with some level of intelligence. To manage the huge amount of heterogeneous data gathered from the different diverse sources, the recourse to AI techniques is a perquisite in order to analzse it and extract valuable knowledge.

We are grateful for the support provided by the many people who contributed to DiCES-N 2020 success. Naturally, the workshop could not take place without the efforts made by the Organizing Committee who helped us to organize and publicize the event, particularly the Technical Program Committee (Sabra Mabrouk, Akka Zemmari, and Soumaya Dahi) and the publicity co chairs (Emna Ben Salem and Rim Negra).

We are also thankful to the members of the Program Committee for providing their valuable time and helping us to review the received papers. We would also like to thank the authors for submitting and then revising a set of high-quality papers. Finally, we express our sincere gratitude to Springer for giving us the opportunity, and we appreciate the support and advice provided by Alfred Hofmann, Amin Mobasheri, and Alla Serikova.

December 2020   Imen Jemili
                                                                  Mohamed Mosbah

Organization

General Chairs

Imen Jemili · University of Carthage, Tunisia
Mohamed Mosbah · Bordeaux INP, France

Program Committee Chairs

Sabra Mabrouk · University of Carthage, Tunisia
Soumaya Dahi · University of Carthage, Tunisia
Akka Zemmari · University of Bordeaux, France

Publicity Co-chairs

Emna Ben Salem · University of Carthage, Tunisia
Rim Negra · University of Mannouba, Tunisia

Program Committee

Salma Batti	University of Carthage, Tunisia
Raoudha Beltaifa	University of Mannouba, Tunisia
Anis Ben Aicha	University of Carthage, Tunisia
Lotfi Ben Othmane	Iowa State University, USA
Kamal E. Melkemi	University of Batna 2, Algeria
Ahmed E. L. Oualkadi	National School of Applied Sciences of Tangier, Morocco
Mohammed Erradi	ENSIAS, Morocco
Parvez Faruki	MNIT Jaipur, India
Matthieu Gautier	University of Rennes 1, France
Tahani Gazdar	University of Jeddah, Saudi Arabia
Fadi Kacem	University of Carthage, Tunisia
Moez Krichen	Albaha University, Saudi Arabia
Bacem Mbarek	Masaryk University, Czech Republic
Neha Pattan	Google, USA
Slim Rekhis	University of Carthage, Tunisia
Ali Safaa Sadiq	Monash University, Malaysia
Gautam Srivastava	Brandon University, Canada
Eiad Yafi	University of Kuala Lumpur, Malaysia
Anis Yazidi	Oslo Metropolitan University, Norway

Contents

Intelligent Transportation Systems

Traffic Congestion Detection: Solutions, Open Issues and Challenges

Ameni Chetouane[1]([✉]) [ID], Sabra Mabrouk[1] [ID],
and Mohamed Mosbah[2] [ID]

[1] Faculty of Sciences of Bizerte, University of Carthage, Tunis, Tunisia
{ameni.chetouane,sabra.mabrouk}@fsb.u-carthage.tn
[2] University of Bordeaux, CNRS, Bordeaux INP, LaBRI, UMR 5800,
33400 Bordeaux, Talence, France
mohamed.mosbah@u-bordeaux.fr

Abstract. In recent years, cities are experiencing a deep negative impact due to traffic congestion. As the number of vehicles is increasing rapidly, traffic congestion becomes unsustainable in urban domains specially in peak hours leading to time and fuel waste, accidents, additional costs for the economy, environmental problems and consequently impaired quality of life. Tremendous effort is done to provide solutions dealing with traffic congestion detection and monitoring. Based on used technologies, existing solutions can be classified into three categories: sensor technology, Vehicular Adhoc Networks and visual traffic surveillance. In this survey, we review the main recent works proposed in each category and discuss their strengths and weaknesses. We give an insight of future directions for handling congestion using the presented methods.

Keywords: Traffic monitoring · Congestion detection · Vehicular Adhoc Networks · Sensor technology · Visual traffic surveillance

1 Introduction

Traffic congestion is a major problem in urban areas, usually caused by a sudden increase in the number of vehicles on the roads during peak hours and the resulting bottlenecks. In fact, even with the continuous improvement of the urban transportation system, the vehicles number tends to increase with the development of the economy, the high population density and the proliferation of ride-share and delivery services [1]. Therefore, road traffic congestion becomes a recurrent problem and has negative impacts on modern society such as economic losses due to waste of time and accidents, environmental problems and health damages due to the increase of CO_2 emissions and noise [2]. The implementation of Intelligent Transport Systems (ITS) attempt to solve or avoid such problems and to provide innovative services related to different modes of transport and traffic management in order to enable users to be better informed and to use transport networks in a safer, better coordinated and more intelligent way [3,4].

© Springer Nature Switzerland AG 2020
I. Jemili and M. Mosbah (Eds.): DiCES-N 2020, CCIS 1348, pp. 3–22, 2020.
https://doi.org/10.1007/978-3-030-65810-6_1

ITS consist of a wide range of applications that process and share information to reduce congestion, improve traffic management, minimize environmental impact and increase the benefits of transport for commercial users and the general public [5]. Many solutions were proposed for traffic congestion detection; based on the adopted technology, they can be classified into three categories: solutions relying on sensor technology, solutions based on Vehicular Adhoc Networks and vision based solutions. In this context, various comprehensive reviews have been presented in the literature. In [6], Dubey and Borkar presented a review study on techniques for detecting and avoiding congestion. For congestion detection, they discussed solutions based on image processing tackling techniques for background and foreground extraction and those applied to aerial images, sensing (inductive loop sensors, magnetic sensors, acoustic sensors) and probe vehicle based techniques, mainly GPS and smartphone based. Moreover, the authors indicate that devices such as GPS is a probe vehicle based technique which can be associated to sensing techniques. The authors in [7] presented a survey on traffic congestion detection and rerouting strategies. They described methods for congestion detection based on fuzzy logic and neural network classifier, during re-routing phase. The authors concluded that the traffic can be minimized using these strategies. In [8], the authors presented a comprehensive review of different methods relative to traffic congestion detection used in video-based traffic surveillance systems. Different systems for traffic congestion detection are presented as well. In [9], a survey of traffic congestion detection using VANET is presented. Two classes of such systems are studied: Infrastructure less solutions based on inter-vehicle communications and infrastructure-based solutions. The authors concluded that the Infrastructure less system based only on Vehicle-to-Vehicle communications is the most powerful option for building traffic system for congestion detection and avoidance. Paranjothi et al. [10] presented a survey of recent congestion detection and control techniques in connected vehicles. They classified congestion detection methods into six categories: measurement-based congestion detection technique, event-driven and priority-based congestion detection technique, Media Access Control (MAC) blocking-based congestion detection technique, cross-layer-based congestion detection technique, dynamic and distributed-based congestion detection technique and location-based congestion detection technique. Then, they identified the drawbacks of existing methods and classified them according to different hierarchical schemes and they recommended solution approaches and future directions for handling congestion in vehicular communications.

We present in Table 1 a comparison of our paper with the other existing survey.

Table 1. A comparison of our paper with the existing surveys

Review	Technology			Content			Years range
	Sensors	VANET	Vision based techniques	Advantages and limitations	Open issues	Challenges	
Dubey and Borkar [6]	✓		✓	✓			1996–2014
Bhandari et al. [7]		✓					2012–2017
Chetouane et al. [8]			✓	✓			2002–2020
El-Sersy et al. [9]		✓					1991–2013
Paranjothi et al. [10]		✓		✓	✓	✓	2003–2020
Our paper	✓	✓	✓	✓	✓	✓	2009–2020

In this study, we present an overview of most relevant proposed solutions for traffic congestion detection while considering classification based on used technology. The contributions of this paper include:

- A classification based on the used technology is adopted with revised sub-categories.
- A review of different methods used for traffic congestion detection including advantages and limitations is presented. We reviewed the most relevant publications up to 2020 and we compare them based on different metrics such as ease of deployment and cost effectiveness, reliability and privacy and security.
- Challenges and some open issues are discussed in order to give an insight on how to overcome the limitations of existing congestion detection approaches.

The paper is organized as follows. In Sect. 2, we present the research methodology. In Sect. 3, we present the different solutions used for traffic congestion detection. Section 4 presents the open issues and challenges. Finally, Sect. 5 draws the conclusion.

2   Research Methodology

The purpose of this comprehensive study is to identify important existing researches related to traffic congestion detection in order to synthesize their respective contributions in this regard. Figure 1 illustrates our methodology in achieving this comprehensive study.

First, we have identified a series of research questions:

- What are the different technologies used for traffic congestion detection ?
- What are their advantages and limitations?
- How can we select an appropriate technology for a specific case?
- What are the open issues and challenges of the different methods?

Obviously, it is possible to ask numerous other questions, but these ones could be sufficient to include a wide range of studies. In the second step, we focus on the following databases to conduct our research: IEEE, Springer, Wiley and Science Direct. The following Key-words were used: "traffic congestion", "traffic

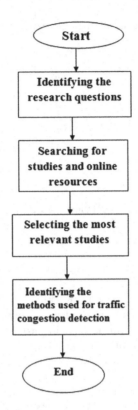

Fig. 1. The methodology used for achieving this comprehensive study

jam", "solution for traffic congestion detection", "VANET", "Vision based", "sensor technology". These search terms were as well combined in order to refine the research. We have selected papers proposing a novel approach for traffic congestion detection, and surveys dealing with this topic, including the most relevant publications up to 2020. We classify them according to techniques and the purpose of research.

3   Solutions for Traffic Congestion Detection

In this section, we present the different solutions used for traffic congestion detection. According to the used technology, three categories can be distinguished: solutions relying on sensor technology, solutions based on Vehicular Adhoc Networks (VANET) and visual traffic surveillance as shown in Fig. 2.

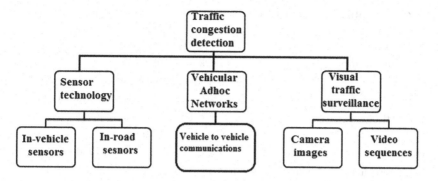

Fig. 2. The different solutions used for traffic congestion detection

3.1   Sensor Technology

Sensor technology has become prevalent in the last decade and has gained a lot of interest. In many domains like smart cities, e-health [11–13], vehicle and traffic monitoring [14], sensors have been deployed . In recent years, sensor technology is widely used to improve road safety and reduce traffic congestion. We can classify sensors into two categories: In-vehicle and In-road sensors [15]. In-vehicle sensors are used to monitor the vehicle performance and status and to provide drivers with greater efficiency and assistance, such as RADAR sensors and GPS, while outside sensors allow to calculate different parameters such as the number of vehicles and traffic density.

In the following, we review the literature about traffic congestion detection for each subcategory. Then, we discuss the advantages and limitations for the different methods.

3.1.1   In-Vehicle Sensors

In ITS, vehicle's sensors can be effective for many applications designed to enhance the driving experience and assist the driver by providing route guidance and parking aids. Some of the most commonly used sensors in vehicles today are shown in Fig. 3.

Fig. 3. Different types of in-vehicle sensors

Table 2. In-vehicle sensors employed in traffic control

Sensor type	Application and usage
Ultrasonic sensors	Parking applications
	Warning applications
	Used for traffic congestion detection
RADAR	Used for collision avoidance
	Safety applications
GPS	Used for traffic congestion detection
Gyroscope and accelerometer sensors	Determine vehicle's position, orientation and velocity

Being equipped with the appropriate sensors is essential to reach the objective of the intended application and reach the desired performance. As summarized in Table 2, only a few sensor can supply many applications with valuable information. However, on sensors are used for traffic congestion detection such as GPS (Global Positioning System) and ultrasonic sensors.

– **Global Positioning System:**
GPS provides accurate and timely information about location and directions, it has been used intensively in many fields. Vehicles equipped with GPS are able to exploit the retrieved information to detect traffic congestion. Andrea and Marcelloni [16] proposed a system for traffic congestion and incidents detection which uses the real-time GPS data. This system is designed to support the traffic management for municipalities and citizens. First, a pre-processed step is applied on GPS traces before placing then in the road map. Depending on vehicle speed, a traffic state is attributed to each road segment. Finally, based on a spatio temporal analysis of classified segments, the system is able to alert users by specifying the concerned area, the estimated speed of vehicles in this area, the traffic status. In [17], Kamran et al. aim to detect incident thanks to real-time data gathered from in vehicle GPS. To this end, each road is divided into segments with a fixed size according to the road type and weather conditions. In order to isolate the potential incident area, segments with an abnormal traffic condition are further divided into smaller segments. In [18], Yoon et al. rely also in GPS data while using speed and time characteristics of road segments in order to extract specific traffic patterns on each road and identify traffic states for each segment. In [19] Gupta et al. exploited GPS traces to model or predict traffic conditions. They proposed a jam detection system able to identify area with regular traffic jams thanks to GPS data extracted from several devices such as mobiles, tablets and vehicles. Using Expectation maximization algorithm, GPS data is first clustered from the devices and the road vehicle data clusters are extracted. Additional processing of these clusters allows to determine the traffic state (congested or light).

– **Ultrasonic sensors:**
  An Ultrasonic sensor is basically a distance measuring sensor and consists of a transmitter unit and an ultrasonic waves receiver unit. When embedded in the vehicle, it emits a sonar allowing to estimate the distance to an object and an alert is triggered once this distance gets smaller than a fixed threshold. An Ultrasonic sensor is also used to detect the speed of the vehicle. In [20], the authors estimate the congestion density in a reliable way. To detect the presence of vehicle queue on the road, a traffic density monitoring module based on ultrasonic sensor nodes (USNs) has to be placed at a predefined distance from the signalized intersections; a module is placed on each side of the incoming road. USN periodically emits the sound wave and, based on the echo received from these transmitted signals, the authors are able to detect the presence of a stationary vehicle on the road, acting as an obstacle. In [21], the authors design a tool for traffic congestion information system on the main road using an Arduino-based ultrasonic sensors. These sensors are used to estimate the speed of vehicles, useful to determine traffic conditions or the situation on a highway. Besides, this type of sensors will provide information for drivers in the form of traffic jam information and other alternative routes, in order to avoid crowded roads. The authors, in [22], use an ultrasonic sensor and a sound sensor to develop a traffic density detection and signal adjustment system to control traffic congestion in urban cities. The ultrasonic sensor is used to detect the density of vehicles. During normal time, the traffic signal timing changes automatically according to the traffic density at the intersection, using ultrasonic. However, when an emergency vehicle is passing, priority is enabled from the feedback of the sound sensor and an override is provided by an instantaneous green signal in the desired direction by blocking the other lanes by red signal.

We present in Table 3 a summary of existing researches using in-vehicle sensors for traffic congestion detection.

Table 3. A summary of different researches using in-vehicle sensors for traffic congestion detection

Article	GPS	Ultrasonic sensor
Andrea and Marcelloni [16]	✓	
Mandal et al. [20]		✓
Kamran et al. [17]	✓	
Prasetyo et al. [21]		✓
Yoon et al. [18]	✓	
Mshelia et al. [22]		✓
Gupta et al. [19]	✓	

Nowadays, vehicles are more and more equipped with a variety of sensors, however the major issue related to this multitude and heterogeneity of sensors is the difficulty of their integration with other components due to the lack of standards generally accepted by the different brands.

3.1.2 In-Road Sensors

Real-time environmental data is gathered by external sensors and then processed to enhance and strengthen transportation networks. These sensors can be divided into two groups according to their location [23].

– Intrusive sensors: These sensors are installed on pavement surfaces such as Inductive loops [15]. Despite their high accuracy, their installation and maintenance are very costly.
– Non-intrusive sensors: These sensors are mounted at different locations on the road allowing to detect several parameters such as vehicle speed [24]. However, they are costly and sensitive to environmental factors.

Currently, several sensors are employed on roads in order to count vehicles number and to classify vehicles or road states. Table 4 presents the different sensors used for traffic congestion detection.

Table 4. Categories of sensors employed for traffic control

Category	Sensor type	Usage
Intrusive	Pneumatic road tube	Vehicle classification Vehicle counting
	Inductive loop detector	Detection of the vehicle's movement Vehicle counting
	Magnetic sensors	Detection of a vehicle's presence Identification of stopped and moving vehicles
	Piezoelectric	Vehicle classification Vehicle counting Measurement of the weight and speed of a vehicle
Non-intrusive	Radar sensors	Speed measurement Detection of the direction of movement of the vehicle
	Infrared sensor	Speed measurement Measurement of length and volume of a vehicle
	Acoustic array sensors	Detection of the presence of a vehicle Speed measurement
	Radio-frequency identification	Tracking vehicles for toll management

As shown in Table 4, one of the most common sensors in traffic management is the Inductive Loop Detector (ILD) which is an intrusive sensor. In [25], a novel inductive loop detector sensor is proposed to allow vehicles detection under an heterogeneous and less-lane disciplined traffic. This loop sensor succeed to detect vehicles of various sizes in any accessible roadway area. The system also enhances the traffic flow information to traffic control commands. Thus, the traffic congestion is detected and an accurate fuzzy based pattern analysis is obtained. In [26], an embedded prototype wireless sensor network system is proposed for traffic congestion detection; the authors developed a communication protocol to exchange traffic congestion information between sensor nodes. This system can be conceived using magnetic sensors for vehicle detection. In [27], the authors develop a new algorithm for traffic density estimation using probe vehicles equipped with various sensors. They develop a methodology to estimate traffic density of a road section by capturing the local densities detected by radar-equipped probe vehicles.

Besides, non-intrusive sensors are also used to detect the traffic congestion such as infrared sensors (IR). In [28], the authors propose a system based on Peripheral Interface Controller (PIC) micro-controller that evaluates the traffic density using IR sensors and accomplishes dynamic timing slots with different levels. Moreover, a portable controller device is designed to solve the problem of emergency vehicles stuck in the overcrowded roads. In [23], Barbagli et al. present an acoustic sensor network, where sensor nodes are placed at road sides, for traffic monitoring. Each sensor node draws a sound map and combines it with an energy detection result to monitor traffic flow distribution. As a huge number of sensor nodes is required at both sides of the road for real time traffic flow monitoring, deployment and maintenance are costly. In [29], the authors determine the blockage at street intersections by utilizing RFID (Radio-Frequency Identification) reader and labels as sensors. The proposed intelligent system adjusts of traffic signals by sensing the density of traffic to minimize the congestion with the help of IoT enabled sensors. The authors, in [30], designed a complete strategy for automatic road traffic congestion detection in real-time using Active RFID and Global System for Mobile Communications (GSM) technology. Since several sensors have been mounted on roads and no proper calibration and cluster integration is available, the collected data is considered unreliable and blocks ITS growth and development.

We present in Table 5 a summary of existing researches using in-road sensors for traffic congestion detection.

In Table 6, we present the advantages and limitations of the different types of sensors.

All kinds of integrated sensors are required to be used by ITS to provide an accurate congestion detection system, combining data from different sensors contributes to make right decision in real time.

Table 5. A summary of different researches using in-road sensors for traffic congestion detection

Article	ILD	IR sensors	RFID	Acoustic sensor	Magnetic sensor	RADAR
Rekha et al. [25]	✓					
Gholve et al. [26]					✓	
Nam et al. [27]						✓
Ghazal et al. [28]		✓				
Atta et al. [29]			✓			
Barbagli et al. [23]				✓		
Roy and Siuli [30]			✓			

Table 6. Advantages and limitations of the different types of sensors

Sensor type	Advantages	Limitations
Inductive Loop Detector	Offers a cost effective solution	High failure rate when mounted in unfavourable road surfaces
Magnetic sensors	Are suitable for deployment on bridges Are not affected by weather conditions	Low sensitivity High consumption
Radar sensors	Are very accurate Easy to install	High susceptibility to electromagnetic interference

3.2 Vehicular Adhoc Networks

Recently, variety of solutions based on Vehicle-to-Vehicle communications were proposed for traffic congestion detection and management [10,31]. Vehicular Adhoc network is a promising technology which enables communication among vehicles. Vehicles must be equipped with On-Board Units to be able to communicate with each other and with the Roadside Units. In the following, we identify the possible types of VANET communications:

– **In vehicle communication:** It detects the internal system data or vehicle performance and determines events such as driver exhaustion or drowsiness etc. Preventing such situations is crucial for public safety as well as driver safety.
– **Vehicle to Vehicle communication (V2V):** V2V communication allows data exchange among vehicles, which is useful for dissemination, safety and security applications. The data exchange between different vehicles assists drivers by informing them about warnings and other critical information [32].
– **Vehicle to road infrastructure communication (V2I):** This type of communication takes place between mobile vehicles and roadside fixed infrastructure in order to gather data. It provides updates related to environmental sensing and monitoring, such as real time traffic updates or weather updates.

- **Vehicle to broadband cloud communication (V2B):** It allows vehicles communication over broadband connections such as 3G/4G and provides the driver with vehicle assistance and tracking, as the broadband cloud may contain more of traffic information and other data [33].
- **Vehicle to Pedestrian communication (V2P):** It allows communication between cars and pedestrians; such communication will be particularly beneficial to elderly persons, school kids and physically challenged persons. V2P may establish a communication between pedestrians smartphones and vehicles and acts as an advisory tool to avoid imminent collisions.
- **Vehicle to Device communication (V2D):** It links cars to many internal devices such as smart-watch, smart-phone and body sensors to monitor the driver health and react when necessary. For example, if the driver is about to feel unwell (blood pressure drop, ...), the car can take the control and navigate to the nearest emergency room. Communication with external devices such as two-wheeled commuters (bicycle, motorbike) is also allowed to exchange mainly safety information [34].
- **Vehicle to Network (V2N):** In this type, Vehicle-capable User Equipment (VUE) and a cloud V2X application server are communicating using V2N services. V2N refers to any contact between vehicles and computer infrastructures, such as Roadside Units (RSU), either deployed with eNodeB or as a standalone UE stationary device [35] as shown in Fig. 4.

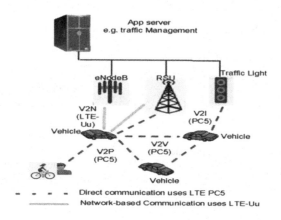

Fig. 4. The VANET communications [35]

Several researches have been focused on detecting and reducing congestion using VANET. Lo and Kuo [36] proposed a method to avoid traffic congestion where every vehicle draws a velocity road map and exchange it with neighbors in order to choose the road with low density. Similarly, the method proposed by Chi et al. [37] aims to detect the average speed and queue length, and then sends this information to the Roadside Units (RSUs). The RSUs receive the information, compare it with the standard threshold, estimate the road condition and then adjust the traffic flow. Finally, the RSUs release the detection results to vehicles, useful for the best path selection. Unfortunately, these methods cannot obtain real-time and accurate traffic information due to vehicles speed motion and limited transmission range. The majority of the existing researches only consider a single factor, mainly velocity, and compare the average speed with a threshold to determine the congestion occurrence, which has been verified to be less accurate and more erratic. Furthermore, there is no quantification of the road condition and traffic congestion. In [38], Cooperative Traffic congestion detECtion (COTEC) is presented. It uses V2V communications and Cooperative Awareness Messages (CAM) or beacon messages to periodically transmit the road traffic condition. Once traffic jam is detected, each vehicle transmits its own evaluation about the traffic jam to collaboratively detect and characterize the road traffic congestion. Similarly, Cooperative vehiculAR Traffic congestion Identification and Minimization (CARTIM) is introduced in [39] and aims to minimize traffic congestion. It also uses V2V communications to cooperatively measure the level of traffic congestion. CARTIM collects data such as speed and density from vehicles and periodically sends it through beacons message to all vehicles and measures the level of congestion using a fuzzy logic system. Once a traffic congestion is detected, CARTIM proposes a heuristic to determine the most appropriate path accordingly.

We present in Table 7 a summary of existing researches using VANET for traffic congestion detection.

Table 7. Summary of the different researches using VANET

Article	Communication level	Tools	Objectives
Bauza et al. [38]	V2V communication	COTEC	Determines and transmits the road traffic condition
Arajo et al. [39]	V2V communication	CARTIM	Minimizes traffic congestion
			Collects data such as as speed and density from vehicles
Cherkaoui et al. [31]	V2V communication	Big data tools	Detects the state of road traffic in urban areas

3.3   Visual Traffic Surveillance

Recently, different researches proposed various traffic congestion detection systems using surveillance cameras. In the following, we distinguish between research studies having considered static images and those analyzing video sequences.

3.3.1   Camera Images

Traffic congestion detection using camera images can be achieved using two approaches. In the first one, the input image can be introduced as an object recognition model to define the number of vehicles in this image; when this number exceeds a predefined threshold, the image can be classified as congested. In this context, authors in [40] proposed to use texture analysis for a real-time road congestion detection system. This later work deals with image data from road surveillance systems and carries out an accurate identification of vehicle density in different scenes. Video frames are initially transformed to 32 level gray images in order to reduce calculations, then four Gray-Level Co-Occurrence Matrix representing horizontal, vertical and diagonal features are computed. Traffic in images can be classified as congested or light using a fixed threshold. The second technique takes as input labeled images as either congested or non-congested. In this context, numerous researchers have used Convolutional Neural Network (CNN) to detect traffic congestion. In general, CNN include a series of convolutional layers separated by activation and pooling layers. They are typically conceived to process the variability of two-dimensional objects as its layers include filters working on two dimensional segments. Activation and pooling layers change the resolution and introduce non linearity. In [41], the authors presented a traffic congestion system initialized with a request sent by a user about traffic condition on a certain location, the system then captures a real time Closed-Circuit Television (CCTV) camera image from the requested location. After that, the system converts the captured image into smaller gray-scale image. A trained CNN model is used to detect the traffic congestion condition and this output is send back to the user as a feedback. The authors in [42], proposed a method for traffic detection using image processing along with object detection. The system extract frames at defined time intervals, then the consecutive frames are compared based on some parameters such as the number of vehicles to determine whether there is a traffic jam.

3.3.2 Video Sequences

Videos sequences are also a frequently used tool to detect traffic congestion. Li et al. [43] presented a new method to detect traffic jams on roads observed from cameras placed on poles or buildings. In this system, an algorithm based on time-spatial imagery is proposed to estimate the road conditions from the video. Experimental results on the estimation of real traffic jams show that the spatio-temporal method is powerful under a complex lighting and traffic environment conditions. In [44], the authors classified traffic congestion into three categories: light, medium and heavy based on the average crowd density and speed of congestion. These approaches depend on handcrafted low-level visual patterns and heuristic rules, thus they have limited ability to deal with complicated crowded scenes. In [45], the authors proposed a congestion detection algorithm in urban intersection using video surveillance. The algorithm is composed of two steps: global vehicle speed detection algorithm and traffic state identification algorithm. The authors took the urban intersection road and selected Region Of Interest (ROI) according to the scene characteristics to improve the processing speed and detection accuracy. Then, they combined two methods: the Shi-Tomasi corner detection algorithm [46] and Lucas-Kanade optical flow method [47] which have strong anti-jamming ability and recognition accuracy. They used the corner points as optical flow tracking points to simplify the calculation and the optical flow to detect and track vehicles in real-time in order to obtain the global vehicle speed and analyze it to determine the road traffic states. In [48], the authors proposed a method to detect the road congestion depending on multidimensional visual features and a Convolutional Neural Network. First, this method detects the different features such as the density of foreground object. The speed of moving object is identified employing optical flow. Then, Gaussian mixture model is used to model the background, and the CNN is employed to precisely identify the eventual foreground from candidate foregrounds. The presented method achieves road congestion detection based on multidimensional feature space, along with traffic density, traffic velocity and road occupancy. However, this method uses background substraction algorithm which considers only single background model to treat several complex behaviors of the background. The authors in [49], proposed a method for road traffic conditions classification into four levels according to the Level of Service (LOS). they used Convolutional Neural Network applied to several traffic video.

3.4 Discussion

Table 8 summarizes the different solutions used for traffic congestion detection which can be classified into three categories: sensors, VANET and visual traffic surveillance. High cost of maintenance and installation, limited range of detection and difficulty in providing real-time traffic information constitute the main shortcomings relative to sensors based techniques [50]. Besides, some types of sensors are sensitive to external conditions such as temperature and humidity, which affect their accuracy. For the VANET technology, the high mobility of vehicles and the dynamic changes of the associated topology in an undeterministic fashion make transmissions over wireless medium very challenging. Besides, V2X message transmission may also be impeded by obstacles such as high buildings near to the streets, leading to packet loss. Apart from this, security is also one of the major issues in VANETs [51]. The third category referring to visual traffic surveillance constitutes an attractive and a cost effective solution, since cameras are cheaper and provide high quality video sequences. However, such a solution is generally sensitive to changes in the acquisition environment like illumination, shadow, weather conditions, etc.

To compare these approaches aiming to detect and monitor traffic congestion, we rely on three metrics:

– **Ease of Deployment and Cost Effectiveness:** The deployment is one of the major issues in sensor technology as a large number of sensor nodes must be deployed to appropriately gather data from the surrounding environment and transmit it to various locations. Besides, deployment and maintenance are very expensive. VANETs deployment is also very expensive as vehicles must be equipped with On-Board Units to communicate with each other and Roadside Units must be installed along roads [52]. For the visual traffic surveillance technique, the deployment is easy as only few cameras can be placed at predefined locations to observe traffic conditions.

- **Reliability:** It refers to the ability of the system components to function under stated conditions. For sensor technology, many factors can affect the performance and the functioning of sensors such as harsh conditions of environments into which sensors are placed, due to their non-traditional locations. Radio propagation in a VANET communication system affects deeply the communication reliability, as wireless channel is prone to errors. Several other factors also impact reliability and latency constraints, specifically the fast changing topology and the low antenna heights.

  For the traffic visual surveillance solutions, several congestion detection methods are sensitive to video quality and the light conditions; they may perform poorly with low resolution videos and low frame rates, such as motion based methods. The performance of these methods decreases when motion information is scarce especially for vehicles appearing only once in a video sequence.

- **Privacy and Security:** Security and privacy are inherent issues to sensor technology and VANET. For example, GPS devices, placed in vehicles, can be used to stalk people without their knowledge. These tracking devices are easy to obtain and may be misused for criminal purposes. Besides, when new cooperative networks systems such as VANETs are deployed, a major concern for users is the loss of privacy, as vehicles can be tracked easily and localized all times. Recent approaches tackling congestion detection in VANETs ignore this important aspect and use unique vehicle IDs that persist over time making it possible for a malicious node to track the location of a vehicle. Along with privacy, security is a legitimate concern for real-world systems, as VANETs and sensor communications are allowed over a shared wireless medium. Moreover, although cameras fixed at roads sides record people's faces and vehicle license plates, This gathered sensitive information remains protected by rules of holding entities.

Table 8. Overview of traffic congestion detection techniques

Technique	Objective	Sensors and approaches	Limitations
Sensor technology	Sensors are inside vehicles	In-vehicle sensors	
		GPS Ultrasonic sensors Electromagnetic sensors	Maintenance and repair Require significant computational cost
	Identify the vehicles using sensors mounted along the road side	In-road sensors	
		Inductive loop sensors Magnetic sensors Acoustic sensors	Subject to effects correlated with installation and environment Concerned by pavement degradation
VANET	Share current local traffic situation information and extract valuable information about traffic congestion	Vehicle to vehicle communications (V2V, V2I..) Cooperative vehiculAR Traffic congestion Identification and Minimization (CARTIM)	Unreliable transmissions through wireless medium Communication overhead
Vision based techniques	Detect traffic congestion using features such as traffic density using images captured from cameras	Camera images	
		Background extraction Foreground extraction	Computational complexity
	Calculate different parameters such as vehicles speed using videos captured from cameras	Video sequences	
		Convolutionnal Neural Network	Sensitive to scene changes due to lighting and surrounding environment

4   Open Issues and Challenges

In this section, we highlight some challenges and open issues that need to be addressed in order to provide efficient methods for traffic congestion detection.

For the sensor technology, a huge amount of data is gathered, so we need the integration of other technologies such as social and mobile networks, data analytic, automated operation tools and decision-making tools to cover all the complete integration requirements from data sensing to sharing in real time. Analyzing data and providing a real time response are challenging since we handle data coming from different and heterogeneous sources. Moreover, many sensitive information related to driver identity and location may be shared which arise many security and privacy issues.

To gather such data, diverse sensing devices are placed on highways, embedded in vehicles and transportation infrastructures, which need to be monitored efficiently; some external factors may obstruct their correct functioning, such as hazardous conditions on roads (e.g. road holes), blurred or erased transit lines or absence of traffic signals. Such situations and factors must be taken into account when designing a traffic congestion detection system based on sensing technology.

For the second solution, VANET has tremendous potential to enhance road safety and offer passengers facilities for a more comfort trip through V2X communications. These communications over a shared wireless medium are exposed to various security attacks, which affects the reliability of the exchanged data and communications. As VANETs offer life-critical road safety applications, security requirements should be satisfied. However, the high mobility of communicating vehicles making securing communications challenging, as contact interval between neighboring vehicles may only last a few seconds, especially in highways. In fact, the volatility where the connectivity between nodes may be very short and temporary, is an intrinsic characteristic of VANETs. Besides, environmental impact must be taken into consideration when designing protocols to ensure security and allow an efficient channel access. For the visual traffic surveillance, there are still major challenges to be overcame. These challenges, including object identification, tracking and analysis, are compounded by practical considerations such as the physical placement of cameras, the network bandwidth required to support them, installation cost, privacy concerns and robustness to unfavourable weather and lighting conditions.

5   Conclusion

In this paper, we have reviewed recent methods for traffic congestion detection and we classified them into three categories : sensor technology, Vehicular Adhoc Networks and visual traffic surveillance. Advantages and drawbacks of each category are highlighted. We can conclude that visual traffic surveillance technique seems an acceptable choice for traffic congestion detection, when considering ease of deployment, cost effectiveness, reliability and privacy and security concerns. To tackle congestion issues, congestion avoidance and detection techniques should be jointly exploited and the recourse to a hybrid technique combining two or more categories should provide a more accurate and robust system. More efforts need to be done to propose architectures and protocols dedicated for such systems.

References

1. Afrin, T., Yodo, N.: A survey of road traffic congestion measures towards a sustainable and resilient transportation system. Sustainability 12(11), 4660 (2020)
2. Sutandi, A.C.: Its impact on traffic congestion and environmental quality in large cities in developing countries. In Proceedings of the Eastern Asia Society for Transportation Studies, vol. 7 (The 8th International Conference of Eastern Asia Society for Transportation Studies, 2009), pp. 180–180. Eastern Asia Society for Transportation Studies (2009)
3. de Souza, A.M., Yokoyama, R.S., Maia, G., Loureiro, A., Villas, L.: Real-time path planning to prevent traffic jam through an intelligent transportation system. In: 2016 IEEE Symposium on Computers and Communication (ISCC), pp. 726–731. IEEE (2016)
4. Chetouane, A., Mabrouk, S., Jemili, I., Mosbah, M.: A comparative study of vehicle detection methods in a video sequence. In: Jemili, I., Mosbah, M. (eds.) DiCES-N 2019. CCIS, vol. 1130, pp. 37–53. Springer, Cham (2020). https://doi.org/10.1007/978-3-030-40131-3_3
5. An, S.-H., Lee, B.-H., Shin, D.-R.: A survey of intelligent transportation systems. In 2011 Third International Conference on Computational Intelligence, Communication Systems and Networks, pp. 332–337. IEEE (2011)
6. Dubey, P.P., Borkar, P.: Review on techniques for traffic jam detection and congestion avoidance. In: 2015 2nd International Conference on Electronics and Communication Systems (ICECS), pp. 434–440. IEEE (2015)
7. Bhandari, A., Patel, V., Patel, M: A survey on traffic congestion detection and rerouting strategies. In 2018 2nd International Conference on Trends in Electronics and Informatics (ICOEI), pp. 42–44. IEEE (2018)
8. Chetouane, A., Mabrouk, S., Jemili, I., Mosbah, M.: Vision-based vehicle detection for road traffic congestion classification. Concurr. Comput. Pract. Exp. 32, e5983 (2020)
9. El-Sersy, H., El-Sayed, A.: Survey of traffic congestion detection using vanet. Commun. Appl. Electron. 1(4), 14–20 (2015)
10. Paranjothi, A., Khan, M.S., Zeadally, S.: A survey on congestion detection and control in connected vehicles. Ad Hoc Netw. 108, 102277 (2020)
11. Zhang, Y., Sun, L., Song, H., Cao, X.: Ubiquitous WSN for healthcare: recent advances and future prospects. IEEE Internet Things J. 1(4), 311–318 (2014)
12. Negra, R., Jemili, I., Belghith, A.: Wireless body area networks: applications and technologies. Procedia Comput. Sci. 83, 1274–1281 (2016)
13. Negra, R., Jemili, I., Belghith, A., Mosbah, M.: MTM-MAC: medical traffic management MAC protocol for handling healthcare applications in WBANs. In: Palattella, M.R., Scanzio, S., Coleri Ergen, S. (eds.) ADHOC-NOW 2019. LNCS, vol. 11803, pp. 483–497. Springer, Cham (2019). https://doi.org/10.1007/978-3-030-31831-4_33
14. Ksouri, C., Jemili, I., Mosbah, M., Belghith, A.: Data gathering for internet of vehicles safety. In 2018 14th International Wireless Communications & Mobile Computing Conference (IWCMC), pp. 904–909. IEEE (2018)

15. Guerrero-Ibáñez, J., Zeadally, S., Contreras-Castillo, J.: Sensor technologies for intelligent transportation systems. Sensors **18**(4), 1212 (2018)
16. D'Andrea, E., Marcelloni, F.: Detection of traffic congestion and incidents from GPS trace analysis. Expert Syst. Appl. **73**, 43–56 (2017)
17. Kamran, S., Haas, O.: A multilevel traffic incidents detection approach: identifying traffic patterns and vehicle behaviours using real-time GPS data. In 2007 IEEE Intelligent Vehicles Symposium, pp. 912–917. IEEE (2007)
18. Yoon, J., Noble, B., Liu, M.: Surface street traffic estimation. In: Proceedings of the 5th International Conference on Mobile Systems, Applications and Services, pp. 220–232. ACM (2007)
19. Gupta, A., Choudhary, S., Paul, S.: DTC: a framework to detect traffic congestion by mining versatile GPS data. In 2013 1st International Conference on Emerging Trends and Applications in Computer Science, pp. 97–103. IEEE (2013)
20. Mandal, A., Sadhukhan, P., Gaji, F., Sharma, P.: Measuring real-time road traffic queue length: a reliable approach using ultrasonic sensor. In: Kundu, S., Acharya, U.S., De, C.K., Mukherjee, S. (eds.) Proceedings of the 2nd International Conference on Communication, Devices and Computing. LNEE, vol. 602, pp. 391–398. Springer, Singapore (2020). https://doi.org/10.1007/978-981-15-0829-5_38
21. Prasetyo, M.A., Latuconsina, R., Purboyo, T.W.: A proposed design of traffic congestion prediction using ultrasonic sensors. Int. J. Appl. Eng. Res. **13**(1), 434–441 (2018)
22. Mshelia, D.E., Alkali, A.H., Dada, E.G., Ismail, K.: Design and development of a traffic density detection and signal adjustment system (2019)
23. Barbagli, B., Manes, G., Facchini, R., Manes, A.: Acoustic sensor network for vehicle traffic monitoring. In: Proceedings of the 1st International Conference on Advances in Vehicular Systems, Technologies and Applications, pp. 24–29 (2012)
24. Yu, X., Prevedouros, P.D.: Performance and challenges in utilizing non-intrusive sensors for traffic data collection (2013)
25. Rekha, R., Karthika, R.: Fuzzy based traffic congestion detection & pattern analysis using inductive loop sensor. Int. J. Sci. Eng. Res. **4**(6), 1149–1152 (2013)
26. Gholve, M.H., Chougule, S.: Traffic congestion detection for highways using wireless sensors. Int. J. Electron. Commun. Eng. **6**(3), 259–265 (2013)
27. Nam, D., Lavanya, R., Yang, I., Jeon, W.H., Jayakrishnan, R: Traffic density estimation using radar sensor data from probe vehicles (2017)
28. Ghazal, B., ElKhatib, K., Chahine, K., Kherfan, M.: Smart traffic light control system. In 2016 Third International Conference on Electrical, Electronics, Computer Engineering and Their Applications (EECEA), pp. 140–145. IEEE (2016)
29. Atta, A., Abbas, S., Khan, M.A., Ahmed, G., Farooq, U.: An adaptive approach: smart traffic congestion control system. J. King Saud Univ. Comput. Inf. Sci. **32**, 1012–1019 (2018)
30. Roy, S.: Real time traffic congestion detection and management using active RFID and GSM technology (2010)
31. Cherkaoui, B., Beni-Hssane, A., El Fissaoui, M., Erritali, M.: Road traffic congestion detection in VANET networks. Procedia Comput. Sci. **151**, 1158–1163 (2019)
32. Dey, K.C., Rayamajhi, A., Chowdhury, M., Bhavsar, P., Martin, J.: Vehicle-to-vehicle (V2V) and vehicle-to-infrastructure (V2I) communication in a heterogeneous wireless network-performance evaluation. Transp. Res. Part C Emerg. Technol. **68**, 168–184 (2016)
33. Tomar, R., Prateek, M., Sastry, G.H.: Vehicular adhoc network (VANET)-an introduction (2016)

34. Al-Fuqaha, A., Kwigizile, V., Oh, J., et al.: Vehicle-to-device (V2D) communications: readiness of the technology and potential applications for people with disability. Technical report, Western Michigan University (2018)
35. Wang, X., Mao, S., Gong, M.X.: An overview of 3GPP cellular vehicle-to-everything standards. GetMobile Mob. Comput. Commun. **21**(3), 19–25 (2017)
36. Lo, C.-C., Kuo, Y.-H.: Traffic-aware routing protocol with cooperative coverage-oriented information collection method for VANET. IET Commun. **11**(3), 444–450 (2017)
37. Chi, J., Do, S., Park, S.: Traffic flow-based roadside unit allocation strategy for VANET. In 2016 International Conference on Big Data and Smart Computing (BigComp), pp. 245–250. IEEE (2016)
38. Bauza, R., Gozálvez, J.: Traffic congestion detection in large-scale scenarios using vehicle-to-vehicle communications. J. Netw. Comput. Appl. **36**(5), 1295–1307 (2013)
39. Araújo, G.B., Queiroz, M.M., de LP Duarte-Figueiredo, F., Tostes, A.I.J., Loureiro, A.A.F.: CARTIM: a proposal toward identification and minimization of vehicular traffic congestion for VANET. In 2014 IEEE Symposium on Computers and Communications (ISCC), pp. 1–6. IEEE (2014)
40. Wei, L., Hong-ying, D.: Real-time road congestion detection based on image texture analysis. Procedia Eng. **137**, 196–201 (2016)
41. Kurniawan, J., Syahra, S.G.S., Dewa, C.K., et al.: Traffic congestion detection: learning from CCTV monitoring images using convolutional neural network. Procedia Comput. Sci. **144**, 291–297 (2018)
42. Nagaraj, U., Rathod, J., Patil, P., Thakur, S.V., Sharma, U., Nagaraj, P.: Traffic jam detection using image processing (2013)
43. Li, L., Chen, L., Huang, X., Huang, J.: A traffic congestion estimation approach from video using time-spatial imagery. In 2008 First International Conference on Intelligent Networks and Intelligent Systems, pp. 465–469. IEEE (2008)
44. Andrews Sobral, L.O., Schnitman, L., De Souza, F.: Highway traffic congestion classification using holistic properties. In: 10th IASTED International Conference on Signal Processing, Pattern Recognition and Applications (2013)
45. Xun, F.-F., Yang, X.-H., Xie, Y., Wang, L.-Y.: Congestion detection of urban intersections based on surveillance video. In: 2018 18th International Symposium on Communications and Information Technologies (ISCIT), pp. 495–498. IEEE (2018)
46. Kadhim, H.A., Araheemah, W.A.: A comparative between corner-detectors (Harris, Shi-Tomasi & FAST) in images noisy using non-local means filter. J. Al-Qadisiyah Comput. Sci. Math. **11**(3), 86 (2019)
47. Bruhn, A., Weickert, J., Schnörr, C.: Lucas/kanade meets horn/schunck: combining local and global optic flow methods. Int. J. Comput. Vis. **61**(3), 211–231 (2005). https://doi.org/10.1023/B:VISI.0000045324.43199.43
48. Ke, X., Shi, L., Guo, W., Chen, D.: Multi-dimensional traffic congestion detection based on fusion of visual features and convolutional neural network. IEEE Trans. Intell. Transpo. Syst. **20**(6), 2157–2170 (2018)
49. Pamula, T.: Road traffic conditions classification based on multilevel filtering of image content using convolutional neural networks. IEEE Intell. Transp. Syst. Mag. **10**(3), 11–21 (2018)
50. Bernas, M., Płaczek, B., Korski, W., Loska, P., Smyła, J., Szymała, P.: A survey and comparison of low-cost sensing technologies for road traffic monitoring. Sensors **18**(10), 3243 (2018)

51. Hasrouny, H., Samhat, A.E., Bassil, C., Laouiti, A.: VANet security challenges and solutions: a survey. Veh. Commun. **7**, 7–20 (2017)
52. Silva, C.M., Masini, B.M., Ferrari, G., Thibault, I.: A survey on infrastructure-based vehicular networks. Mob. Inf. Syst. **2017**, 6123868 (2017)

Pollution Context-Aware Representation in Vehicular Internet of Things for Smart Cities

Twahirwa Evariste[1]($\boxtimes$), Willie Kasakula[1], James Rwigema[1], and Raja Datta[2]

[1] African Center of Excellence in IoT, College of Science and Technology-University of Rwanda, P.O.Box 3900, Kigali, Rwanda
e.twahirwa@ur.ac.rw
[2] Department of Electronics and Electrical Communication Engineering, Indian Institute of Technology Kharagpur, Kharagpur 721302, India

Abstract. The present era is associated with remarkable urban developments that have attracted migrants from rural to urban areas for various reasons, hence overpopulated cities. This leads to the increased congestion, air pollution, and other high population density related problems that could threaten the lives of urban commuters. With the current materialization of the Internet of Things, and smart city development, context-aware and pervasive computing are deemed to gain paramount consideration through sensing and actuating technologies. In this research work, we introduce a vehicular IoT pollution context-aware representation system. Firstly, In-vehicle pollution context-aware system is suggested that targets two key pollutants, i.e Carbon-dioxide CO_2 and Particulate Matter $PM_{2.5}$. Most importantly vehicles having many passengers on-board are monitored for these two pollutants of concern. Once their levels exceed the allowable limits, end-users that are truly concerned should be alerted and mitigation measures are taken. Secondly, vehicular entities are observed in the area of interest, and their gaseous emissions are thought to be the major sources of air pollution. This explains why keeping a sharp eye on each vehicle's level of pollutants in its emissions is equally important. Drivers and environmental monitoring personnel could be informed of the abnormal levels of some key pollutants such as NO_x, NH_3, CO_2, and so forth. While the CO_2 and $PM_{2.5}$ monitoring is conducted using on-shelf sensors, an intra-vehicular pollution context-aware system is designed and developed that automatically operates an electric fan that could be deployed to control the level of temperature and pollutant's level in vehicular environments.

Keywords: Context-aware system · Vehicular-IoT · Pollution context

1 Introduction

With the materialization of the Internet of things, real-world physical entities could be equipped with sensing, computation, communication, and to some

Supported by ACEIoT.

I. Jemili and M. Mosbah (Eds.): DiCES-N 2020, CCIS 1348, pp. 23–39, 2020.
https://doi.org/10.1007/978-3-030-65810-6_2

extent with some level of intelligence. Furthermore IoT has seamlessly enabled physical and digital worlds to interact through sensory, radio identification, and actuation technologies, (Sethi and Sarangi 2017); (Khan et al. 2017); (Mazhelis et al. 2012); (Li et al. 2015). The IoT has been utilized in various sectors including smart city scenarios, smart manufacturing, smart health, smart grid, and so forth, (O'Connor, n.d.); (Reka and Dragicevic 2018); (Yang and Tsung 2019). Prolonged exposure to polluted environments may be a source of numerous health problems like cardiac health conditions, lung diseases, asthma, and so forth. In urban environments transportation has been revealed as one of the prominent sources of air pollution, especially fossil fuel CO_2 releases that are the major contributor to climate change (Patil 2017). Some of the major alarming pollutants in Rwanda Include: NOx, SO_2, $PM_{2.5}$, CO_2, CO, of which most of them are found in vehicles gaseous emissions. Commuters could be exposed to increased levels of transportation-related air pollution, due to the fact that they are much closer to vehicular emissions. While more efforts have been put forward in monitoring vehicles emissions that cause air pollution, (Moutinho 2020); (Kaivonen and Ngai 2020) it is worthwhile very crucial to keep a sharp eye on key pollutants in the intra-vehicular environments, most importantly public buses, and other sorts of vehicles that carry a big number of passengers at once such as organizational vans, etc.

1.1   Context-Aware Presentation in Vehicular IoT

The concept of context-awareness representation has been a challenging factor in vehicular-environments due to the rapid pace of the entities participating in vehicular networks (Vahdat-Nejad 2016). Context in vehicular networks

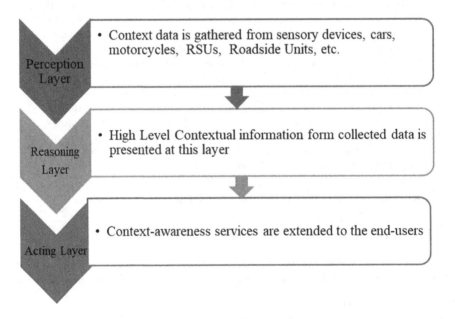

Fig. 1. Generalized context-aware architecture

describes an instantaneous situation, this includes vehicle locations, in-vehicle micro-environments, vehicular neighborhood, and so forth. The architecture of a typical context-aware system is based on three layers; the perception or sensing layer, the reasoning layer, and the acting layer. Figure 1 portrays the three layers of a context-aware architecture

- The perception layer collects contextual information from different sensors; in vehicular context-aware systems, these sensors may be intra-vehicle (e.g. Chemical detecting sensors, acceleration, acoustic sensors, and other sensors that monitor intra-vehicle micro-environments) and so forth or be deployed in the vehicle's surroundings (e.g. Air pollution, temperature, relative humidity, etc.) to gather the data of interest.
- The Reasoning layer handles data processing activity to obtain high-level context-aware information, e.g. The driver's fatigue is detected based on the driver's inattention, acceleration-deceleration variations, and other driving behaviors. Driving behaviors greatly influence traffic situations.
- Last but not the least is the acting layer, it is at this layer that services are extended to the end-users that are truly concerned with a particular context-awareness system, in the aspects of the internet of vehicles user include drivers, passengers, pedestrians or even other vehicles that have got common interests. Relevant decisions are taken based on the context-aware system interests.

The intent of this work is to implement an IoT-based real-time pollution context monitoring in vehicular environments i.e in-vehicle pollution monitoring and exhausted emitted gases from vehicular entities of target. Most importantly, key pollutants will be monitored in intra-vehicular environments like public buses that have many passengers onboard, while motorcycles, Cars, Vans, and Trucks will be monitored for the amount of pollution they contribute to the neighborhood environments. We summarize the contributions of this paper as follows:

- Pollution context-aware vehicular IoT system is designed and implemented to control the key pollutants inside vehicle environments and levels of pollution in emitted gases.
- We implement an advisory mechanism to alert the concerned user whenever key pollutants exceed the allowable limits.
- Specifically for the intra-vehicular environment as a proof of concept, an automated blowing system is implemented that is instantly triggered to blow fresh air in and polluted air out from vehicular environments to ensure the comfort of passengers on board. The blower works on an actuation basis and needs no human intervention in its operation.

The rest of this paper is organized as follows: Sect. 2 surveys the works that are closer to ours. We introduce the target area, traffic types and volumes in Sect. 3. Section 4 highlights the proposed vehicular IoT context-aware architecture and required materials to develop the system. We present the results in Sect. 6 and conclude our work in Sect. 7. In the next section, we conduct a literature survey of works that broadly explain the concept of vehicular air pollution monitoring.

2   Related Work

The field of vehicular context-aware representation has been a popular topic in both research, and the automotive industry, and has been in existence for several years. Specifically ensuring context-awareness in smart vehicular environments, drivers encounter complex interactions, like the vehicles they are driving, other vehicles, and the environment. As far as transportation-related air quality is concerned, the peak traffics flow normally coincides with the higher concentration of air pollutants in the area of peak traffics (Sun et al. 2019). For instance, the levels of air pollutants dropped drastically during the lock-down due to the pandemic. This is mainly because the human activities related to air pollution decreased as most of the people were forced to stay home. But observations indicate that as the economy of numerous countries start to recover, the levels of pollution in many countries are returning to pre-covid19 levels (Berman and Ebisu 2020); (Tanzer-Gruener et al. 2020); (Budd and Ison 2020); (Economist-2020 2020, n.d.).

Generally speaking, context-awareness systems are the systems that are cognizant of the environments, they sense and adapt to the environments (Engelenburg et al. 2019). With the assist of the Internet of Things, context-aware systems are able to collect data from heterogeneous objects that interact with human beings, physical surroundings, and so forth. The confluence of IoT and context-aware systems have seamlessly allowed different important application domains. In (Francesco and Angelo 2017), an IoT context-aware system is studied that supports a cultural heritage operations, the deployed sensors, Information communication technologies in cultural heritage environments such as museums, art exhibition are integrated with IoT based context-aware systems that improve the quality of services offered at such places and introduce a smart cultural heritage environments.

Moreover, the IoT based context-awareness has been useful in handling smart health-related context. Authors in (Amna Pir 2015) learn an IoT context-awareness architectural framework for health management information systems (HMIS). A context-awareness middle-ware system is introduced that helps manage the patients' information. Whereas an IoT based ambient intelligent system is introduced through context-awareness. Environmental contextual information gathered from sensory devices are used to explore contexts and end-user preferences. Context-aware computing is considered the most important part of ubiquitous computing, and communications. The alterations in the context are utilized as the inputs to the context-aware systems and actions are taken based on the context changes. A context-aware computing air health monitoring system is suggested in (Banani and Zeenat 2020) that helps to inform on the nature of the air in urban scenarios. Air pollutants of interest are sensed and ultimately alerts are triggered using context information once threatening levels of air pollution are captured. Additionally, the progressive development in the actuation technologies has boosted a wide range of adoption of transportation pollution monitoring and control.

A context-aware E-Bike research study is suggested in (Sweeney et al. 2018), which reduces pollution inhalation in the cycling process. The objective of this study is the control of cyclist ventilation rate through the use of electric motor assistance. A cyber-physical control system is introduced that reduces the impacts of town pollution on a cyclist.

With the introduction of autonomous vehicles, the technological advancement in vehicular context-awareness has been also advancing. For instance, context-aware object detection and identification techniques would enable autonomous vehicles to seamlessly use the roads (Guo and Guizani 2019). Furthermore, context-awareness in vehicular Ad Hoc networks is enhanced by integrating and aligning knowledge. Context-awareness is very crucial in the semantic web of things as this ensures better and structured context data demonstration. The work in (Ruta and De Vera 2018) learns a new framework that supports contextual information management and mining in Vehicular Ad Hoc Networks based on a knowledge fusion algorithm.

In the current era of cognitive computing, The context-awareness domain is applicable in numerous areas, for instance in the new technology of augmented reality, system users are able to interact with the real-world environments with the help of digital information. Furthermore, in (Sun and Li 2020) authors assert a novel accident prevention mechanism based on context-awareness mechanism while operating mobile phone. Their research work defines the context-awareness system into three-fold sub-problems i.e human behavior awareness sub-problem, the geographical position sub-problem, and interactive awareness sub-problem.

Some vehicular context-aware systems are very crucial and need to some extent a certain level of security and privacy. Since vehicular contexts change as vehicles move from point to point along the roads, it becomes tricky to consistently capture their context-representation. Ensuring their security becomes an issue as well. For example, making certain that the speed of a self-driven vehicle is not tempered by an intruder is of great importance. This is possible if the context-awareness of that vehicle is constantly monitored. The work in (Tian et al. 2016) suggests a securing context-awareness in Vehicular Ad Hoc Networks. Their research work proposes a technique that counts the level of security from the state transition probability. The method in this work estimates the probability of the vehicle to stay in a secure state. Vehicular Contextual information gathering such as vehicle speed, vehicular traffic density, and others provides plenty of benefits. In (Amjad Zubair and Muhammad 2016) a context-aware data aggregation in Vehicular Ad-hoc Networks is presented based on vehicular speed and traffic density and ensures a downsized communication cost in terms of channel bandwidth.

Even-though numerous research works have been conducted in pollution monitoring, but air pollution monitoring in micro-environments like intra-vehicular environments and level of pollutants in the vehicular emitted gases. In this paper, we design and implement a low-cost pollution monitoring and control that targets micro-environments like intra-vehicular environments and the level of pollution in vehicular gaseous emissions. The developed system has a couple of advantages, firstly it runs on a long-range low power wide area network protocol. Furthermore, the developed system could be extended to other indoor environments that are extremely sensitive to polluted air.

3   Target Area Demonstration, Traffic Types, and Sizes

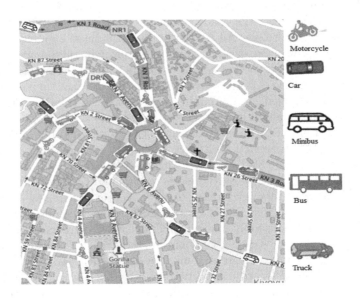

Fig. 2. Area of interest representation

To fully understand the levels of impact several vehicular entities may cause or encounter, we have learned various sorts of vehicles in the area of interest, the target area is shown in Fig. 2, this will be our initial are for pollution context-aware system deployment. The levels of cumulative contribution of pollution in the area are obviously proportional to the population of entities. The area considered, is part of downtown-Kigali city. The instant total number of vehicular agents is assumed from six individual routes in the target area, all main routes, daily traffic volumes are demonstrated in Figs. 3a, b, c, d, e, f.

Transportation related air pollutants saturation is based on the number of the vehicular agents that are emitting polluted gaseous emissions. In our target area traffic flows information is recorded after every 15 min. Not every vehicle is emitting polluted gases, however the entire contribution of all vehicles in the area will have impact on the ambient air. It is obvious that the most affected routes will be the ones with heavy traffic volumes, and this motivates the environmental monitoring officials to determine the most vulnerable ares that could mostly be hit by transport related pollution. If S represents a set of pollutants to be collected and monitored in a specific area, and $S = s_1, s_2, s_3 \ldots s_m$ For instance the total transportation related pollution concentration P_{r1tot} in a specific route r of the target area will be given by the following equation:

$$P_{r1tot} = \left[Pv1_{1,2,3,...m} + Pv2_{1,2,3,...m} + ... + Pvm_{1,2,3,...m} \right].$$ (1)

Where $Pv1_{s_{1,2,3,...m}}$ = The pollution produced by vehicular entity V_1, $Pv2_{s_{1,2,3,...m}}$ = The pollution produced by vehicular entity V_2, $PvN_{s_{1,2,3,...m}}$ = The pollution produced by N^{th} vehicular entity

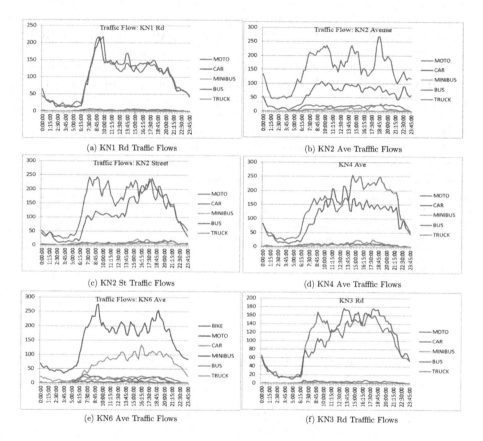

Fig. 3. Area of interest representation and traffic types

While the above scenario in Eq. 1 describes air pollution saturation in a single route of consideration, Eq. 2 could be employed to estimate the accumulation of pollution in a specific area of a collection of routes. In this case, we are estimating the total transport related pollution P_{Total}, where m pollutants are being monitored in an area of r routes. From the target area, we observe that the value of r is 6, and the overall pollution accumulation will be calculated as shown in Eq. 2 based on the individual vehicular pollution as shown in Eq. 1.

$$P_{Total} = \sum_{i=1}^{r} \sum_{j=1}^{m} P_{ij} \tag{2}$$

In this scenario, to understand the overall pollution concentration in our area, P_{Total} is given by $P_{r1total} + P_{r2total} + \ldots + P_{r1total}$, P_{Total} is the total pollution accumulation produced by vehicular objects in route r_1. The first term in Eq. 3 implies the level of pollutants that a vehicle v_1 produces in route r_1 while the second term in the same equation stands for the pollution contribution by vehicle v2 in the same route respectively. If for instance, we have n vehicles in the rout the last term signifies the pollutants emitted by the $n^t h$ vehicle.

The same technique is employed in the rest of the routes under considera-tion. Equation 4 indicates the overall pollution gathering concerning all entities in route 2 Pr2tot, in the target area. Likewise, Pr3tot represents the overall con-tribution of vehicular entities in route 3 as stated in Eq. 5. Generally speaking, we intend to indicate the sum of the transport-related air pollution based on the specific number of vehicular entity numbers in specific routes under the region of interest. Equations 3, 4, 5, 6, 7, 8 state the total pollution that could be gathered in route1, route2,route3,route4,route5, and route6 respectively. Most importantly, this is applicable to any nth for m pollutants to be monitored. The simplified model is very crucial to estimate the overall pollution that may arise in a specific area, and mitigation measures could be set as well. For N routes that have n vehicles, a collection of pollutants could be determined by summing the equations below.

$$P_{r1tot} = \left[Pv1_{r1_{1,2,\ldots m}} + Pv2_{r1_{1,2,\ldots m}} + \ldots + Pvn_{r1_{1,2,\ldots m}} \right]. \tag{3}$$

+

$$P_{r2tot} = \left[Pv1_{r2_{1,2,\ldots m}} + Pv2_{r2_{1,2,\ldots m}} + \ldots + Pvn_{r2_{1,2,\ldots m}} \right]. \tag{4}$$

+

$$P_{r3tot} = \left[Pv1_{r3_{1,2,\ldots m}} + Pv2_{r3_{1,2,\ldots m}} + \ldots + Pvn_{r3_{1,2,\ldots m}} \right]. \tag{5}$$

+

$$P_{r4tot} = \left[Pv1_{r4_{1,2,\ldots m}} + Pv2_{r4_{1,2,\ldots m}} + \ldots + Pvn_{r4_{1,2,\ldots m}} \right]. \tag{6}$$

+

$$P_{r5tot} = \left[Pv1_{r5_{1,2,\ldots m}} + Pv2_{r5_{1,2,\ldots m}} + \ldots + Pvn_{r5_{1,2,3,\ldots m}} \right]. \tag{7}$$

+

$$P_{r6tot} = \left[Pv1_{r6_{1,2,\ldots m}} + Pv2_{r6_{1,2,\ldots m}} + \ldots + Pvn_{r6_{1,2,\ldots m}} \right]. \tag{8}$$

4   Methodology and Materials

This study learns two important scenarios for air pollution environments. Firstly, in-vehicle environments are monitored for the levels of two key pollutants i.e Carbon dioxide (CO_2), and Particulate matter ($PM_{2.5}$). Secondly, we monitor the level of air pollution in the emitted gases from vehicles. Figure 4 shows the suggested pollution context monitoring system in this study. Two important LoRa compliance sensors are employed to monitor pollutants that saturate inside vehicle environments. I.e, LS-111P and LS-113G., the sensors deployed for pollutant monitoring operate at 5 V. While the vehicles are moving the dedicated sensors could be powered by the moving car's engines with a Micro-USB DC power-in, 5 V. Alternatively, mini-solar panels of 5 V could power the sensing device once properly deployed on the vehicles. The sensors are employed to monitor CO_2 and $PM_{2.5}$ in real-time mode. $PM_{2.5}$ has been a target pollutant of interest for monitoring in numerous countries (Chen et al. 2017); (Huang and Kuo 2018). With the introduction of novel aerial technology, particulate matter could be monitored using unmanned aerial vehicles. Airborne particulate matters that are harmful to human being are monitored in the concepts of smart cities (Gao et al. 2020).

$CO - 2$ has been another important pollutant that is normally monitored to ensure a clean environment where gas emissions are so high like in industrial, urban areas, transportation-related, and ect. The trend of the internet of things has been helpful in achieving air quality monitoring study goal, and most importantly in environment monitoring (Ali et al. 2015); (Duangsuwan et al. 2018) For in-vehicle environments monitoring, public buses that have a big number of passengers on-board are of the target, the aim is to monitor some key pollutants, and control their accumulations inside vehicles that have multiple people onboard. This will reduce the risk of commuters that spend more time ins public buses on a regular basis to acquire air pollution related-diseases.

Moreover, pollutants from the vehicles emitted gases could spread and affect all people that are in the proximity of vehicles. In this context, most people that are in vulnerable positions include: motorists, road works employees, road cleaners, pedestrians, and etc. While private cars and motorcycles are the dominating entities in the target area, they normally carry few or no passengers. However, they contribute a lot to the road air pollution, we therefore introduce a low cost IoT-based vehicular pollution context monitoring in vehicular emissions. The vehicular pollution context monitoring system suggested in this study is based on the general IoT three-tier architecture, which mainly consists of three main layers. i.e Perception layer, Network layer, and application layer. The perception layer is the low-level layer that includes physical sensing nodes, actuators, and etc. The physical parameters of concern are sensed and captured at this level. Specifically, in our work, air pollution monitoring sensors are found at the level. CO_2, $PM_{2.5}$, MQ135 sensors are utilized to monitor air pollution in both intra-vehicular environments, and level of pollutants in the vehicular gaseous emissions.

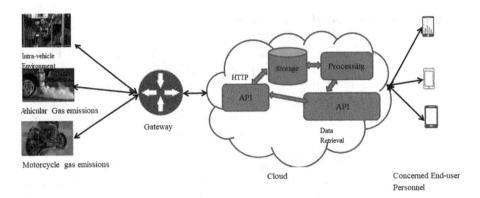

Fig. 4. Proposed VIoT pollution context monitoring

The network layer contains communication protocols that manage the transmission of sensed parameters to the end-users. In IoT architectures, it is possible to find multiple IoT supported protocols such as LoRa, NB-IoT, Bluetooth, Z-wave, Zigbee, and etc. coordination techniques are important at this level to harmonize the heterogeneity in the protocols. A loRa based gateway is employed that accepts data from multiple sensory devices to the internet. An IMST Lite Gateway is employed that is an eight-channel based on iC880A concentrator and a raspberry Pi. The configured gateway is based on 868 868 MHz radio band, a license-free spectrum that is reserved for Industrial, Scientific and Medical applications. The third layer is the application layer, a high-level layer that enables data processing, and presentation. Air pollution data collected in our scenario are retrieved at the application layer. Visualization techniques are implemented here. Triggers for notifications are also set.

4.1   LoRa Signal Power

To ensure the performance of the system, the quality of the signal is learnt, the based position of the gateway is decided based on the routes of vehicles to be monitored so that the signal quality is enough to deliver the target parameters. Analytical log-distance path loss modeling technique is employed to make sure the received signal power is enough for data transfer. Since the received signal power decreases logarithmically with the distance between the sensing device and the gateway, Eq. 9.

$$\mathbf{P}_L(d_{g,s}) = P_{Tx} - P_{Rx} = P_L(d_0) + 10m \log_{10}(d_{g,s/d_0}) + X_\sigma \tag{9}$$

$P_L(d_{g,s})$ = Transmission Power (P_{tr})- Received Power(P_r), $d_{g,s}$, is the distance that determines a good communication signal between the sensors deployed in the vehicles under consideration. m is the path loss exponent, its value varies based on the environmnet, while X_σ is the normal random variable with zero mean. Generally, the received signal power will depend on the spreading factor (Lavric and Popa 2018), and spreading factors differ based on the euclidean distance between the communicating devices. But based on the positions of the vehicles under consideration, the transmitted data is received with a high signal quality. Figure 5 demonstrates the route of the target vehicles that were monitored for this particular work. The lora gateway was deployed at the quarters of the University of Rwanda, College of Science and Technology, an indoor. Initially, the gateway is deployed closer to the route of interest, however, for the entire region monitoring optimal configuration of the gateways will be required.

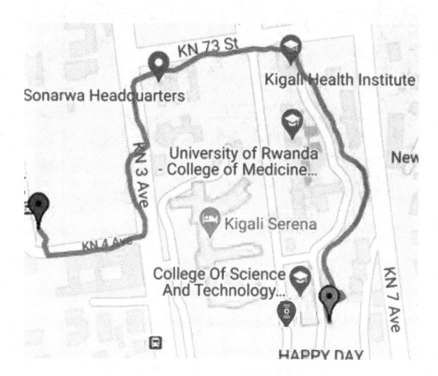

Fig. 5. The route of the monitored vehicles

5   IoT Based Vehicular Context Collection Device Prototype

In this section, we introduce an IoT low-cost device that could be employed for vehicular context collection monitoring and representation. While this section emphasizes on inside vehicle monitoring, the device could be used to detect the levels of pollutants in the vehicular gaseous emissions. The main purpose of the device Fig. 6 is to monitor the intra-vehicular context. It is designed to monitor the temperature, humidity, carbon dioxide (CO_2) and, ammonia (NH_3) inside the vehicles that carry many passengers at a time like public transport buses. The devices uses a DHT sensor to monitor the temperature and humidity, and an MQ135 sensor to monitor the NH_3 and CO_2. These sensors are connected to a NodeMCU micro-controller which collects data from the sensors then upload them to a server. The NodeMCU is based on the ESP8266 wi-Fi, a system on chip that enables developed device to be connected to the internet.

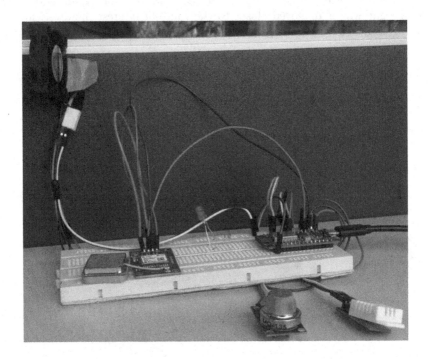

Fig. 6. IoT based pollution monitoring device

Before uploading to the sensor, however the NodeMCU checks the levels of NH_3 and CO_2 and compare them to the set thresholds of for CO_2 and NH_3. If any of the two values are above the set thresholds, an electric fan connected to the same NodeMCU is automatically actuated with the purpose of reducing the levels of the pollutants of interest, and cools the environments. It is only when the levels of both NH_3 and CO_2 are below the threshold that the fan is turned off. Furthermore, the values of all the four parameters are uploaded to a server for persistence. This data is concatenated with a number plate parameter for identification of the exact vehicle where the data was collected from. The server runs an API that receives the sensor data in JSON format then adds a time component before inserting it into a database to know when data was collected. It also provides a user interface which tabulates all the data from the database on users' request Fig. 7.

Timestamp		Number Plate		Temperature		Humidity		CO2		NH3	
Fri, 11 Sep 2020 13:22:27 GMT		RAE 503W		26.8		69.9		1.96		3.13	
Fri, 11 Sep 2020 13:22:35 GMT		RAE 503W		26.8		70.4		2.04		3.25	
Fri, 11 Sep 2020 13:22:42 GMT		RAE 503W		26.8		70.1		2.02		3.22	
Fri, 11 Sep 2020 13:22:50 GMT		RAE 503W		26.8		69.7		2.05		3.26	
Fri, 11 Sep 2020 13:22:57 GMT		RAE 503W		26.8		69.7		1.96		3.13	
Fri, 11 Sep 2020 13:23:05 GMT		RAE 503W		27		70.2		2.02		3.22	
Fri, 11 Sep 2020 13:23:12 GMT		RAE 503W		26.5		69.2		2.05		3.26	
Fri, 11 Sep 2020 13:23:20 GMT		RAE 503W		26.7		70.2		1.75		2.84	
Fri, 11 Sep 2020 13:23:27 GMT		RAE 503W		27		70.2		2.08		3.3	
Fri, 11 Sep 2020 13:23:35 GMT		RAE 503W		26.8		69.8		2.04		3.25	
Fri, 11 Sep 2020 13:23:42 GMT		RAE 503W		26.8		70.1		2.04		3.25	
Fri, 11 Sep 2020 13:23:50 GMT		RAE 503W		26.8		69.8		1.74		2.83	
Fri, 11 Sep 2020 13:23:57 GMT		RAE 503W		27.1		69.8		1.73		2.81	
Fri, 11 Sep 2020 13:24:05 GMT		RAE 503W		27.3		69.9		2.04		3.25	
Fri, 11 Sep 2020 13:24:12 GMT		RAE 503W		26.7		69.4		2.03		3.23	
Fri, 11 Sep 2020 13:24:20 GMT		RAE 503W		26.7		69.3		2.03		3.23	
Fri, 11 Sep 2020 13:24:27 GMT		RAE 503W		26.9		69.7		1.99		3.18	
Fri, 11 Sep 2020 13:24:35 GMT		RAE 503W		27		70.3		1.96		3.13	
Fri, 11 Sep 2020 13:24:42 GMT		RAE 503W		26.7		69.3		2.02		3.22	
Fri, 11 Sep 2020 13:24:50 GMT		RAE 503W		26.8		70.2		2.03		3.23	

First Prev 3 4 5 6 7 Next Last

Fig. 7. IoT based pollution monitoring data

6   Results Presentation

6.1   Real Time Readings and Notifications

As pointed out above, this paper focuses on two-fold applications, i.e in-vehicle, and emitted gaseous pollution context collection and demonstration. In this subsection, we present inside vehicle pollution monitoring, specifically, CO_2 and $PM_{2.5}$ Figs. 8 (a) and (b) demonstrate the in-vehicle real-time pollutants monitoring. Having knowledge about the concentration of key pollutants in vehicular environments will save the lives of passengers that regularly spend more time on-board Figs. 11 (a) and (b). Most importantly, we enable the concerned users to trace the pollutants in different time lengths based on the applications, daily, weekly, monthly pollution context-parameters could be retrieved.

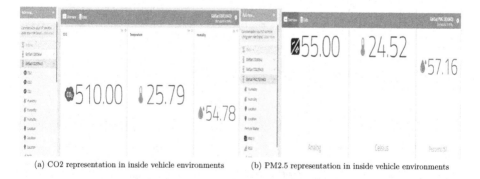

(a) CO2 representation in inside vehicle environments   (b) PM2.5 representation in inside vehicle environments

Fig. 8. CO_2 and $PM_{2.5}$ real time monitoring

While the above two figures demonstrate real-time monitoring of the CO_2 and $PM_{2.5}$ respectively, in Fig. 9 (a) and (b), we highlight the continuous on-board monitoring of the two key pollutants for a week time. We set thresholds to alert drivers in case of pollution surges. During the monitoring period, peak readings were observed while more passengers are on-board. And this calls for constant pollution monitoring in public buses pollution monitoring. Interestingly our proposed system enhances the historical monitoring of a particular vehicle. Through an intuitive web-based dashboard each vehicle's historical status could be retrieved based on a day, weekly, monthly, and so forth. Constant monitoring of the vehicle will allow persistence in setting up mitigation measures. The target pollutants are monitored along with vital weather parameters like intra-vehicular temperature, and humidity as presented in Fig. 10 (a) and (b) respectively. A combination of intra-vehicular and emitted gaseous pollution monitoring could help in keeping clean urban vehicular environments and the city in general. Figure 7 demonstrates the data collected by the prototype device. Each monitored vehicle is uniquely identified by the vehicle plate number. The work presented in this paper will be extended to ensure data handling and privacy. Once the vehicle's internal environment is associated with much pollution or levels of pollutants in the emitted gases go beyond the allowable levels, the same vehicle is identified and the owner, driver, or environmental monitoring personnel should be notified to take quick followup. For instance, if the problem is due to mechanical issues, they should be fixed. Time context is very crucial to understand when anything happened. For instance in Figs. 9 (a) and (b), 10 (a) and (b), pollution and weather parameters fluctuate. It is very important to understand when the levels of pollution increase, decrease, and why. In our observations, the monitored pollutants saturation rises when several passengers are on board, especially the levels of carbon dioxide. The device prototype and is employed to monitor CO_2 is NH_3 whereas global sat sensors are utilized to monitor the levels of CO_2 and $PM_{2.5}$.

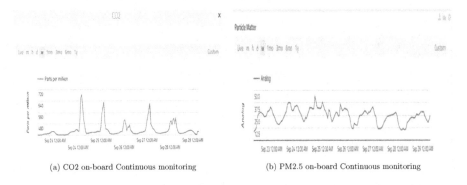

(a) CO2 on-board Continuous monitoring   (b) PM2.5 on-board Continuous monitoring

Fig. 9. CO_2 and $PM_{2.5}$ on-board continuous monitoring

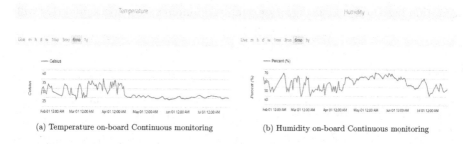

(a) Temperature on-board Continuous monitoring

(b) Humidity on-board Continuous monitoring

Fig. 10. Temperature and PHumidity on-board continuous monitoring

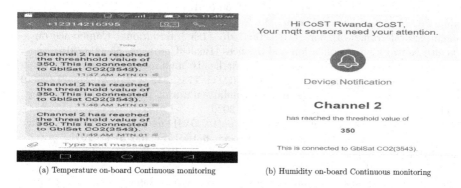

(a) Temperature on-board Continuous monitoring

(b) Humidity on-board Continuous monitoring

Fig. 11. Pollution alerts to the end-users

7   Conclusion and Future Work

In this study, we developed a pollution context-aware vehicular IoT based system for both intra-vehicle and vehicular gaseous emissions. When the levels of pollutants under consideration go beyond allowable limits, concerned users are notified for suitable mitigation measures. Most importantly for intra-vehicles that have many passengers on-board, we have introduced an IoT-based pollution context-aware system with an automated electric fan that is activated to reduce the temperature and levels of contaminants without human being's intervention. Notifications are transmitted to the concerned users whenever the level of pollutants surpasses the allowable limits. Under the case study area, the developed system will be deployed in numerous vehicular entities under consideration i.e motorcycles, cars, minibuses, buses, and trucks, and the transportation-related air pollution concentration in a target area will be monitored based on the traffic types that dominantly move regularly in that area. While this research work is limited to the pollution context collection and representation in vehicular environments as well as emitted gaseous pollution, handling voluminous data from many devices deployed in vehicles and the privacy of the collected data is very crucial. This guides us in the future research direction, handling voluminous data and the privacy of this data from very many sources like vehicular entities will be our next research focus. Understanding the accumulation of pollution saturation based on vehicle density would be an interesting aspect, and this will be in the scope of our future research work.

References

Ali, H., Soe, J.K., Weller, S.R.: A real-time ambient air quality monitoring wireless sensor network for schools in smart cities. In: 2015 IEEE First International Smart Cities Conference (ISC2), pp. 1–6 (2015)

Amjad Zubair, A.K.J., Song, W.C., Muhammad, S.: Context aware data aggregation in vehicular ad- hoc networks. In: Noms 2016–2016 IEEE/IFIP Network Operations and Management Symposium, pp. 1257–1260 (2016)

Amna Pir, M.A.K., Usman Akram, M.: Internet of Things based context awareness architectural framework for HMIS. In: 2015 17th International Conference on e-health Networking, Application and Services (HealthCom), pp. 55–60 (2015)

Banani, G., Zeenat, R.: A mechanism for air health monitoring in smart city using context aware computing. Procedia Comput. Sci. **171**(2512–2521), 2512–2521 (2020)

Berman, J.D., Ebisu, K.: Changes in US air pollution during the COVID-19 pandemic. Sci. Total Environ. **739**(139864), 139864 (2020)

Budd, L., Ison, S.: Responsible transport: a post-COVID agenda for transport policy and practice. Transp. Res. Interdisc. Perspect. **6**(100151), 100151 (2020)

Chen, L., et al.: An open framework for participatory PM2.5 monitoring in smart cities. IEEE Access **5**, 14441–14454 (2017)

Duangsuwan, S., Takarn, A., Jamjareegulgarn, P.: A development on air pollution detection sensors based on NB-IoT network for smart cities. In: 2018 18th International Symposium on Communications and Information Technologies (ISCIT), pp. 313–317 (2018)

Economist-2020: Air pollution is returning to pre-covid levels (n.d.). https://www.economist.com/graphic-detail/2020/09/05/air-pollution-is-returning-to-pre-covid-levels

van Engelenburg, S., Janssen, M., Klievink, B.: Designing context-aware systems: a method for understanding and analysing context in practice. J. Log. Algebr. Methods Program. **103**, 79–104 (2019)

Francesco, P., Angelo, C.: The Internet of Things supporting context-aware computing: a cultural heritage case study. Mob. Netw. Appl. **22**(2), 332–343 (2017)

Gao, J., Hu, Z., Bian, K., Mao, X., Song, L.: AQ360: UAV-aided air quality monitoring by 360-degree aerial panoramic images in urban areas. IEEE IoT J. (2020)

Guo, J., Song, B., Chen, S., Yu, F.R., Du, X., Guizani, M.: Context-aware object detection for vehicular networks based on edge-cloud cooperation. IEEE IoT J. (2019)

Huang, C.-J., Kuo, P.-H.: A deep CNN-LSTM model for particulate matter (PM2.5) forecasting in smart cities. Sensors **18**(7), 2220 (2018)

Moutinho, J.L., et al.: Near-road vehicle emissions air quality monitoring for exposure modeling. Atmos. Environ. **117318** (2020)

Kaivonen, S., Ngai, E.C.H.: Real-time air pollution monitoring with sensors on city bus. Digit. Commun. Netw. **6**(1), 23–30 (2020)

Khan, A.A., Rehmani, M.H., Rachedi, A.: Cognitive-radio-based Internet of Things: applications, architectures, spectrum related functionalities, and future research directions. IEEE Wirel. Commun. **24**(3), 17–25 (2017)

Lavric, A., Popa, V.: Performance evaluation of LoRaWAN communication scalability in large-scale wireless sensor networks. Wirel. Commun. Mob. Comput. **2018** (2018)

Mazhelis, O., Luoma, E., Warma, H.: Defining an Internet-of-Things ecosystem. In: Andreev, S., Balandin, S., Koucheryavy, Y. (eds.) NEW2AN/ruSMART -2012. LNCS, vol. 7469, pp. 1–14. Springer, Heidelberg (2012). https://doi.org/10.1007/978-3-642-32686-8_1

Patil, P.: Smart IoT based system for vehicle noise and pollution monitoring. In: 2017 International Conference on Trends in Electronics and Informatics (ICEI), pp. 322–326 (2017)

Reka, S.S., Dragicevic, T.: Future effectual role of energy delivery: a comprehensive review of internet of things and smart grid. Renew. Sust. Energy Rev. **91**, 90–108 (2018)

Ruta, M., Scioscia, F., Gramegna, F., Ieva, S., Di Sciascio, E., De Vera, R.P.: A knowledge fusion approach for context awareness in vehicular networks. IEEE IoT J. **5**(4), 2407–2419 (2018)

Sethi, P., Sarangi, S.R.: Internet of Things: architectures protocols and applications. J. Electr. Comput. Eng. **2017**(1–0147), 1–014 (2017)

Li, S., Da Xu, L., Zhao, S.: The Internet of Things: a survey. Inf. Syst. Front. **17**(2), 243–259 (2015)

Sun, B., Li, Q., Guo, Y., Li, G.: Context awareness-based accident prevention during mobile phone use. IEEE Access **8**, 27232–27246 (2020)

Sun, X., Chen, H., Su, X.: Analysis of pollutant distribution based on taxi travel volume: a case comparison of Xi'an and Ningbo, China. In: 2019 5th International Conference on Transportation Information and Safety (ICTIS), pp. 765–772 (2019)

Sweeney, S., Ordonez-Hurtado, R., Pilla, F., Russo, G., Timoney, D., Shorten, R.: A context-aware e-bike system to reduce pollution inhalation while cycling. IEEE Trans. Intell. Transp. Syst. **20**(2), 704–715 (2018)

Tanzer-Gruener, R., Li, J., Eilenberg, S.R., Robinson, A.L., Presto, A.A.: Impacts of modifiable factors on ambient air pollution: a case study of COVID-19 shutdowns. Environ. Sci. Technol. Lett. **7**(8), 554–559 (2020)

Tian, X.Y., Liu, Y.H., Wang, J., Deng, W.W., Oh, H.: Computational security for context-awareness in vehicular ad-hoc networks. IEEE Access **4**, 5268–5279 (2016)

Vahdat-Nejad, H., Ramazani, A., Mohammadi, T., Mansoor, W.: A survey on context-aware vehicular network applications. Veh. Commun. **3**, 43–57 (2016)

Yang, H., Kumara, S., Bukkapatnam, S.T., Tsung, F.: The Internet of Things for smart manufacturing: a review. IISE Trans. **51**(11), 1190–1216 (2019)

O'Connor, Y., Rowan, W., Lynch, L., Heavin, C.: Privacy by design: informed consent and internet of things for smart health (n.d.)

ROI Extraction for Intrusion Detection in Platooning Join Maneuver

Haifa Gharbi$^{(\boxtimes)}$ and Sabra Mabrouk

Faculty of Sciences of Bizerte, University of Carthage, Tunis, Tunisia
{haifa.gharbi,sabra.mabrouk}@fsb.u-carthage.tn

Abstract. In the context of platooning, a high degree of cooperation between platooning members is required to perform major maneuvers. One of the most challenging issues is to perform join-maneuver due to the strong interference caused by unintended vehicles entering in the middle during this maneuver. In order to detect and identify vehicles (unintended or not) during a join maneuver, we propose a vision based solution allowing to observe the front area of the platooning member, track and identify newly joined vehicles. In this paper, we focus on delineating this region of interest (ROI) by extracting road lanes in video sequences from on-board cameras in the platooning vehicles. The performance of our method is tested and validated using videos of highway scenes in different weather conditions (sunny, rainy, cloudy).

Keywords: Platooning · Join-maneuver · Road lane extraction · Edge detection · Region of interest

1 Introduction

Thanks to the advancement of automobile technology and the progress in vehicular ad-hoc networks (VANET), car platooning have been attracting attention of several vehicle manufactures and research academia [1]. A platooning, also known as a road train, can be defined as a group of vehicles traveling together in the same lane at the same speed while maintaining a relatively small inter-vehicle distance. It is composed of a leader, which is the first vehicle of the platooning driven by a human, and one or more followers, called platooning members. The leader acts as a chief and the vehicles behind react and adapt to changes in its movement, such as braking, lane changing, etc. The leader is responsible for keeping the stability of the entire platooning by specifying the suitable speed, distance between vehicles and the appropriate direction to follow; this information is communicated to all the members. This functional behaviour allows improving road capacity and on-road safety, reducing energy consumption and pollution and, most crucial in charge of executing basic maneuvers. The leader orchestrates the different maneuvers such as join, leave, split, merge, etc. In join maneuver, platooning members collaborate in order to leave a gap for an authorized vehicle to join the platooning. During the leave maneuver, any member can

© Springer Nature Switzerland AG 2020
I. Jemili and M. Mosbah (Eds.): DiCES-N 2020, CCIS 1348, pp. 40–52, 2020.
https://doi.org/10.1007/978-3-030-65810-6_3

exit the platooning whenever it reaches its destination for example. The Merge maneuver consists of joining two platoons driving on the same lane. In extreme cases, a platooning can be divided into two, it is the split maneuver. When the leader decides to leave, the platooning will be dissolved.

Performing any maneuver e.g. merge or split requires powerful and effective communication between platooning members in order to ensure the operation efficiency and safety. One of the major problems is to perform join-maneuver by an unintentional or unauthorized vehicle i.e. joining in the middle during the platooning fusion maneuver. In this context, authors in [2] analyzed the interference that may be caused by an unintentional vehicle during the joining maneuver. Although they did not provide a solution, they identified four scenarios that could interrupt this operation. The most critical one refers to car interference occurring whenever a human-driven car occupies the gap vacated for the authorized vehicle. Authors in [3] proposed an algorithm to identify the interference caused by an unintended vehicle getting in the opened gap instead of the authorized. The main idea is to split the platooning at the intrusion point and then merge sub-platoons. In order to verify the identity of the new member and to ensure a successful termination of the operation, the authors compare the radar distance with the GPS position, broadcasted by the authorized vehicle, to identify the vehicle entering the gap of platooning. If no matching, an intrusion is detected. Such a solution is limited by the precision and availability of GPS data and the reliability of wireless communications [4].

Our objective is to propose a new solution to detect and identify vehicles (unintended or not) during a join maneuver by analyzing video sequences from embedded cameras in the platooning vehicles. Each platooning member will be able to locally detect intrusions without any interaction with the leader or the other vehicles. We consider a platooning of trucks traveling along a highway and each truck is equipped with a front camera allowing observing the region of interest (ROI), tracking and identifying newly joined vehicles; the ROI is the front area of the truck. In this paper, we propose a method to identify the ROI of the road area extracted in front of the truck by analyzing the video stream of the front-view camera.

The reminder of this paper is organized as follows: Sect. 2 gives an overview of lane detection techniques. The details of the proposed method are described in Sect. 3. Experimental results and validation are presented in Sect. 4. Finally, Sect. 5 summarizes this work.

2   State of the Art

A common approach for vehicle detection and tracking over time is to delineate a region of interest (ROI) to restrict the area to be observed. Relying on road lines detection is an effective way to proceed. In this context, several methods, based on video sequences or images, have been proposed over years. In this section, we provide an overview of related works on lane detection and delimitation of the region of interest.

Lane detection is one of the most fundamental and challenging problems in platooning. It aims to find, from a digital image or video flow, the white or yellow horizontal lane marking on the painted road surface. This deduced lane marking can be useful for obstacle and lane change detection, accident avoidance, driver intention monitoring to maintain his safety, etc. In this context, authors in [5] proposed to detect lane markers using images from two downward side cameras installed on the front and rear of the vehicle. This work aims to ensure that vehicles run straight along the lane by estimating its lateral position and its yaw angle to a lane. The first step of this method consists in extracting candidate points of lane markers by edge pair detection. Hough transform is then applied to these candidate points in order to detect straight lines representing lane markers. The lateral position in the traffic lane is estimated based on the straight-line position in the image of each camera. By using these lateral positions and the distance between the two downward side cameras, the yaw angle towards the traffic lane can be calculated. Cameras position is the major limitation of this method as downward side cameras have a narrow field of view and only a small amount of lane information can be captured. Authors in [6] also exploited images captured from a front-view camera to detect road lane markings in order to support surveillance and autonomous driving. These images are passed into a semantic segmentation network based on U-Net architecture to extract the characteristics of road lane markings. Then, Hough transform method is used to find lines. Finally, in order to get rid of unnecessary detected lines, K-means clustering is applied to calculate the most suitable line for each road lane marking. Although the proposed system succeeds in fairly detecting straight lines, it fails when dealing with curves. Authors in [7] proposed a lane detection algorithm based also on Hough transform. First, the lane markings are extracted by applying a one-dimensional ridge detector to each row of the image. Then, the Hough transform is used to detect the different lines.

Edge detection is another method that allows identifying points where the brightness of an image changes sharply. In [8], Canny edge detector is applied to obtain the edge of lane markings in road images, where only areas with useful information are considered. Lanes are then detected using Hough transform technique. Similarly to [6], curved lines remain an unresolved issue. In [9], the authors proposed a lane departure warning system for real-time lane detection and monitoring. This algorithm takes images acquired by forward-facing in-car cameras as input to detect the two lanes closest to the vehicle (left and right). Even if one lane is obstructed, the segmented ends of the last image are used to estimate the next lane. However, this method cannot accurately detect lines occulted by any objects such as pedestrians or vehicles, and it is too slow to provide cars with real time information. In [10], the authors proposed a method using the vanishing point to detect lines. As only parallel road lanes have to pass through a vanishing point in the image plane, they are able to filter other irrelevant detected lines. A probabilistic voting procedure based on the strength of the line segment is adopted to estimate the vanishing point from a noisy image. Then, a score function is defined to estimate lanes. Finally, the flooding watershed algorithm is used to detect lanes.

In recent years, deep neural network (DNN) technology has been widely used in various applications. In [11], LaneNet, a DNN based method, was proposed for lane detection. Images obtained from the front-view camera are processed to generate a lane edge proposal map, useful for inferring the location of lanes in the image.

3   Proposed Method

In order to allow each truck in the platooning to check and confirm any newly introduced platooning member, the basic idea is to enable platooning trucks to keep an eye on the front area where vehicles could be inserted. In this paper, we aim to find the ROI bounding the road area in front of the truck through analysing video stream from a front-view camera.

Various lane detection methods have recourse to edges detection in order to extract all linear structures in the image [8,12,13]. However, applying such a technique on the whole image leads to irrelevant lines identification, as shown in Fig. 1. Therefore, we first proceed with a road extraction step in order to avoid such noise. To this end, we exploit color feature relative to the road since its color is commonly in gray shades while lane markers are white or yellow. Then, we detect lines within the extracted road area. As illustrated in Fig. 2 our approach requires three steps: road extraction, lane detection and ROI identification.

Fig. 1. Noise in lane detection.

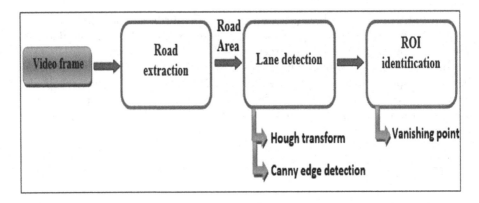

Fig. 2. Overview of the proposed method.

3.1 Road Extraction

Road extraction is an important step in our method, it helps cleaning the scene for the following steps. It mainly allows enhancing the lane detection process. Exploiting the color feature, considered as one of the robust features which allows detecting objects in an image efficiently and rapidly [14,15], we apply a thresholding to frames based on a color range in the road gray shades. This color range is empirically fixed as the road color is similar worldwide.

As depicted in Fig. 3, many unwanted gray objects could be detected in the image, such as trees, sky in bad weather conditions, other vehicles, etc. This may cause false recognition in the lane detection step. In order to overcome this problem, it is necessary to isolate the road area by removing all unnecessary other gray objects.

(a)   (b)

Fig. 3. (a) Original image, (b) Obtained objects after applying thresholding.

To this end, we start labelling the connected components in the binary image resulting from thresholding. The road region is identified as the largest connected component area from the labeled image (Fig. 4(a)). Then, morphological transformations are applied to smooth the detected area and get rid of holes as shown in Fig. 4(b). The final result of road extraction is exposed in Fig. 4(c).

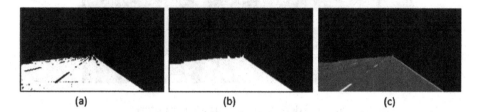

Fig. 4. Road isolation: (a) Before morphological transformations; (b) After morphological transformations (c) Final result.

3.2 Lane Detection

Before applying the edge detection operator, the Gaussian filtering is employed in our method in order to smooth the image and remove noise. Then, Canny edge detection is used to extract edges in the selected road zone; it estimates gradient to detect pixel intensity changes [8]. After that, given the binary edge image, lane detection is obtained through Hough transform which is a widely deployed technique to detect lines in images [16]. It performs straight lines detection defined by Eq. 1:

$$\rho = x\cos(\theta) + y\sin(\theta). \tag{1}$$

Where

- ρ represents the distance from the line to the origin of the coordinate system,
- θ represent the angle between the normal line and the x-axis,
- x and y represent the pixel coordinates of the line.

As shown in Fig. 5, the lanes marked in red color are detected using Hough transform. These lanes represent the solid and dashed white lanes on the extracted road area.

Fig. 5. Lane detection using Hough transform.

3.3   ROI Identification

Once the lanes are detected, they can be easily extended by estimating their equations expressed by:

$$y = mx + b. \tag{2}$$

where m represents the slop and b represents the y-intercept. In fact, since all extracted lines are at an angle to the horizontal, they have a linear slope.

Extended lines could have many intersection points, we selected, in our case, the vanishing point with the maximum number of lines passing through as shown in Fig. 6.

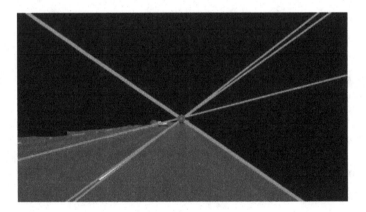

Fig. 6. Extended lanes and vanishing point (green circle). (Color figure online)

The triangle area in front of the vehicle represents the targeted region of interest (ROI); this region can usually be used for vehicle and obstacle detection.

It is defined with three points: the vanishing point and two other ones resulting from the intersection of a drawn horizontal line (yellow line in Fig. 7) with two detected lanes.

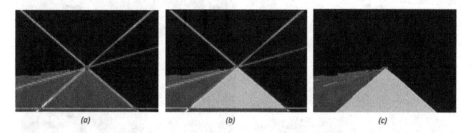

Fig. 7. ROI identification: (a) Intersection with horizontal line, (b) Triangle area, (c) Final result. (Color figure online)

4   Experimental Results

In this section, we evaluate our method for lane detection and ROI extraction using different metrics, the used dataset contains video sequences from diverse highways, the presumed context of platooning.

4.1   Dataset

We gathered 80 online video sequences captured using front-view cameras in highway scenes from different cities (California, Turkey, Texas, Toronto, Seoul-Korea, Marysville-usa). We classify these videos sequences into four categories based on weather conditions (sunny, rainy, snowy and cloudy), they include straight roads with solid and dash lines. Table 1 summarizes the used dataset details and Fig. 8 gives some examples of the used highway scenes.

Table 1. The used dataset description.

	Sunny	Rainy	Cloudy	Snowy
Number of video sequence	30	20	20	10
Duration(s)	50			
Frame rate (fps)	30			
Resolution	960 × 540			

Fig. 8. Used highway scenes: (a) sunny day, (b) rainy day, (c) cloudy weather, (d) snowy day

4.2   Evaluation Metrics

In our case, positive data refers to the correct lane point while negative one refers to the non-lane point. Thus, the following rates could be defined:

- False positive (FP) rate referring to the correct detected lanes,
- False negative (FN) rate giving missing lanes
- True positive (TP) rate representing the number of falsely detected lanes.

The computation of these quantities is obtained with reference to a manually created ground truth data. Since no negative data (i.e., ground-truth non-lane point) can be delimitated, (TN) rates are 0%. Therefore, in order to validate the performance of our method, we focus on the following metrics:

- **Recall rate:** Measures the proportion of lanes that have been correctly detected. It is calculated as follows:

$$Recall = \frac{TP}{TP + TN}. \tag{3}$$

- **Precision rate:** measures the proportion of positive lanes actually detected. It is expressed by:

$$Precision = \frac{TP}{TP + FP}. \tag{4}$$

- **F-measure:** Is the average of precision and recall, it is computed as follows:

$$F - measure = 2 \times \frac{Recall \times Precision}{Recall + Precision}. \tag{5}$$

4.3   Results

Figure 9 shows some ROI detection results (green triangle) in different weather conditions. Our method partially fails to detect lines, resulting in a visually misplaced region of interest. As we can see, detection results seem quite good for sunny days (Fig. 9(a) and (b)), while they are less satisfying in cloudy and rainy weathers (Fig. 9 (c), (d) and (e)). Our method partially fails to properly detect lines, resulting in a visually misplaced ROI (Fig. 9 (f)).

Table 2 shows the computed recall, precision and accuracy rates according to the different considered weathers conditions.

Table 2. The proposed method performance according to weather conditions.

	Sunny %	Rainy %	Cloudy %	Snowy %
Recall	93	63	71	23
Precision	99	64	88	18
F - measure	96	63	78	20

We can notice that our method gives excellent results on sunny days with rates exceeding 90% for the three considered metrics; these results are expected since, in such conditions, lane marks are clearly recognizable. In cloudy days, the proposed method maintains acceptable results. However, in rainy scenes, due to the interference of raindrops on the front windshield, the performances are degraded with F-measure, recall and precision rates slightly above 60%. In snowy weather, our method gives lower percentages with only 20% for F-measure, 23% for recall and 18% for precision. This could be explained by the fact that in such circumstances, the road is totally or partially covered with white snow which distorts the road extraction and lane marks detection and leads to an increased false-positive number.

Fig. 9. Result of ROI detection in different weather conditions: (a), (b) sunny day; (c), (d) rainy day; (e) cloudy weather; (f) snowy weather (Color figure online)

5   Conclusion

Our main objective through this research is to exploit a visual based solution in the context of platooning in order to ensure the well execution of a join maneuver. To delineate the tracking zone where newly joined members can be inserted, we present in this paper a ROI identification method based on road lane extraction. This method includes three main steps: road extraction based on color feature, edge detection using Canny and lane detection by applying the Hough transform. Intersection between detected lanes allows delimitating the targeted ROI. Experimental results show that the proposed method performs well under good weather conditions and gives acceptable rates in cloudy weather. However, under severe conditions (rain and snow), noise and false detection may occur. As future work, we intend to investigate the proposed method performances according to the variability in road conditions and distortions in lane marking. Moreover, further experiments and improvements are required to ascertain the effectiveness of our method in curved roads.

References

1. Bergenhem, C., Shladover, S., Coelingh, E., Englund, C., Tsugawa, S.: Overview of platooning systems. In: Proceedings of the 19th ITS World Congress, Vienna, Austria, 22–26 October (2012)
2. Segata, M., Bloessl, B., Joerer, S., Dressler, F., Cigno, R.L.: Supporting platooning maneuvers through IVC: an initial protocol analysis for the JOIN maneuver. In: 2014 11th Annual Conference on Wireless on-Demand Network Systems and Services (WONS), pp. 130–137. IEEE, April 2014
3. Paranjothi, A., Atiquzzaman, M., Khan, M.S.: PMCD: platoon-merging approach for cooperative driving. Internet Technol. Lett. 3(1), e139 (2020)
4. Hoang, G.M., Denis, B., Härri, J., Slock, D.T.M.: Distributed link selection and data fusion for cooperative positioning in GPS-aided IEEE 802.11 p VANETs. Proc. WPNC 15, 1–6 (2015)
5. Kasai, T., Onoguchi, K.: Lane detection system for vehicle platooning using multi-information map. In: 13th International IEEE Conference on Intelligent Transportation Systems, pp. 1350–1356. IEEE, September 2010
6. Tran, L.A., Le, M.H.: Robust U-Net-based road lane markings detection for autonomous driving. In: 2019 International Conference on System Science and Engineering (ICSSE), pp. 62–66. IEEE, July 2019
7. Kuk, J.G., An, J.H., Ki, H., Cho, N.I.: Fast lane detection & tracking based on Hough transform with reduced memory requirement. In: 13th International IEEE Conference on Intelligent Transportation Systems, pp. 1344–1349. IEEE, September 2010
8. Yan, X., Li, Y.: A method of lane edge detection based on Canny algorithm. In: 2017 Chinese Automation Congress (CAC), pp. 2120–2124. IEEE, October 2017
9. Dong, Y., Xiong, J., Li, L., Yang, J.: Robust lane detection and tracking for lane departure warning. In: 2012 International Conference on Computational Problem-Solving (ICCP), pp. 461–464. IEEE, October 2012
10. Yoo, J.H., Lee, S.W., Park, S.K., Kim, D.H.: A robust lane detection method based on vanishing point estimation using the relevance of line segments. IEEE Trans. Intell. Transp. Syst. 18(12), 3254–3266 (2017)
11. Wang, Z., Ren, W., Qiu, Q.: Lanenet: real-time lane detection networks for autonomous driving. arXiv preprint arXiv:1807.01726 (2018)
12. Daigavane, P.M., Bajaj, P.R.: Road lane detection with improved canny edges using ant colony optimization. In: 2010 3rd International Conference on Emerging Trends in Engineering and Technology, pp. 76–80. IEEE, November 2010
13. Low, C.Y., Zamzuri, H., Mazlan, S.A.: Simple robust road lane detection algorithm. In: 2014 5th International Conference on Intelligent and Advanced Systems (ICIAS), pp. 1–4. IEEE, June 2014
14. Chetouane, A., Mabrouk, S., Jemili, I., Mosbah, M.: Vision-based vehicle detection for road traffic congestion classification. Pract. Exp. Concurr. Comput., e5983 (2020)

15. Chetouane, A., Mabrouk, S., Jemili, I., Mosbah, M.: A comparative study of vehicle detection methods in a video sequence. In: Jemili, I., Mosbah, M. (eds.) DiCES-N 2019. CCIS, vol. 1130, pp. 37–53. Springer, Cham (2020). https://doi.org/10.1007/978-3-030-40131-3_3
16. Duan, D., Xie, M., Mo, Q., Han, Z., Wan, Y.: An improved Hough transform for line detection. In: 2010 International Conference on Computer Application and System Modeling (ICCASM 2010), vol. 2, pp. V2–354. IEEE, October, 2010

Emerging Networking Technologies

Secure, Context-Aware and QoS-Enabled SDN Architecture to Improve Energy Efficiency in IoT-Based Smart Buildings

Akram Hakiri[1]([✉])(iD), Bassem Sallemi[1,2](iD), Fatma Ghandour[3](iD), and Sadok Ben Yahia[2,4](iD)

[1] SYSCOM ENIT, ISSAT Mateur, University of Carthage, Tunis, Tunisia
`akram.hakiri@enit.utm.tn, sellami.bassem@gmail.com`
[2] Faculty of Sciences, Department of Computer Sciences, University of Tunis El Manar, Tunis, Tunisia
`sadok.benyahia@fst.rnu.tn`
[3] Planning Department, Tunisie Telecom, Les jardins du Lac II, 1073 Tunis, Tunisia
`fatma.ghandour@tunisietelecom.tn`
[4] Tallinn University of Technology, Akadeemia tee 15a, Tallinn, Estonia

Abstract. Nowadays, buildings are increasingly energy intensive, as they represent almost 40% of total energy consumption and more than 35% of CO_2 emissions. The excessive and unnecessary use of planet resources and the use fossil fuel and a non-renewable energy source urged government and industry to explore new research directions and utility-driven energy improvement programs to drive advances in energy-efficient. Energy efficiency in smart buildings can be achieved by introducing a context-aware Internet of Things (IoT) approach, where sensors can learn from their surrounding environment to control the actuators in a coordinated network. However, the IoT network requirements are constantly changing in unpredictable fashion, which needs faster and frequent on-demand network reconfiguration. Software Defined Network (SDN) has been envisioned as a new approach to enable a flexible and agile network programmability in diverse IoT scenarios. However, the focus has primarily been on the design of the SDN computation logic, i.e. controllers, while the dynamic delivery and operations service-inferred IoT resource allocation has been postponed.

To address this plethora of challenges, this paper we first extend Software Defined Network (SDN) with Network Function Virtualization (NFV) to support distributed IoT sensing devices automation and orchestration in micro-grid data center at the network edge of smart campus building. Second, we introduce a novel IoT data management model based on data-centric middleware IoT message broker that implements a hierarchical containment tree for retrieving sensor data from remote IoT devices. Then, we introduce a context-aware knowledge learning approach that maps raw sensing data into a meaningful context and transform them into the appropriate context representation models. Finally, we provide a proof of concept to demonstrate successful deployment and provisioning of virtualized services in the context of Smart Campus research project.

Keywords: Energy efficiency · Smart building · Software defined networking · Internet of Things · Context-awareness · Service Function Chaining

© Springer Nature Switzerland AG 2020
I. Jemili and M. Mosbah (Eds.): DiCES-N 2020, CCIS 1348, pp. 55–74, 2020.
https://doi.org/10.1007/978-3-030-65810-6_4

1   Introduction

Energy consumption has increased drastically at global scale due to the growing urbanization in cities. Buildings account nearly 40% of the global energy consumption [4,5] and more than 35% of CO2 emissions [1] in many countries. Governments and industry are exploring new research directions and utility-driven energy improvement programs to drive advances in energy-efficient, by motivating the awareness of society to become energy conscious and adopt energy conservation and energy efficiency measures, and developing micro-grids systems that can be managed intelligently to save energy within a building or even within a city. Despite the promise, recent behavioral studies [26] have shown that it is still a challenging issue to incentive human behavior from an energy perspective [22]. For example, in campus housing and residential education buildings, which represent 9% of operating micro-grids [9], users are often unaware that changing their daily routines, e.g. doing laundry by night or setting at maintenance temperature their Heating Ventilation and Air-Conditioning (HVAC) equipment's, turning off unnecessary lighting and projectors, etc. could impact their energy consumption patterns. Consequently, achieving energy efficiency goals despite the challenges of changing users habits becomes a key challenging issue.

The proliferation of diverse Internet of Things (IoT) technologies such smart meters, embedded sensing and networking at various levels of power grids, which makes it possible to achieve energy saving and information sharing among sensing devices and actuators [31]. However, because power-grids generate enormous amounts of raw data from different zones in buildings, these data embrace uncertainty and imperfection due to the inaccuracies and imprecision inherent in data sources. That is, in order to implement an efficient smart energy management system, collected data should be reasoned to unearth knowledge and reflect a meaningful context [23]. The context-awareness should be used to react and trigger specific events to change the behavior of IoT devices, e.g. automating and adapting the indoor lighting, closing curtains, switching off the light, ensure the comfort level by controlling the HVAC equipment's, etc.

Additionally, the heterogeneous and dynamic aspects of IoT sensors generating these raw data pose major challenges for the underlying network by requiring support for handling heterogeneity, dynamic changes, device discovery as well as context-awareness. Aggregating heterogeneous sensory data from different types of sources needs an agile infrastructure that embraces message brokers, sensor virtualization and softwarization for flexible, cost-effective, secure, and private IoT deployment for diverse applications and services. Existing standardized communication protocols [12], such as IEC 61850, IEEE P1547.8, and Modbus, are designed in isolation to solve a specific problem and are often retrofitted to address a new requirement. They often lack the right abstractions that address the interoperability requirements of IoT communication. Thus, if network resource utilization is a concern, the network must be flexible enough to be reprogrammed in accordance with any change in IoT application needs. Current network provisioning approaches neither address the dynamicity of IoT applications nor care about resource utilization.

To address these key challenges, there is a need to enhance the future micro-grids industry through intelligence to enable a successful deployment and realization of powerful and trusted IoT networks. Software Defined Network (SDN) [7,11,25] and

Network Function Virtualization (NFV) [2,30] show a significant promise in meeting micro-grids communication needs. SDN can achieve fine-grained resource management, enforce traffic forwarding policies and keep the micro-grid network overhead as simple and minimal as possible. SDN can also solve interoperability issues in smart micro-grids communication, as it can deal with heterogeneous devices exchanging data formats and diverse protocols for M2M data exchange. It can also improve cooperation and capability mismatch between IoT devices to handle simultaneous connections of various communication technologies. With the help of NFV, SDN can virtualize a set of network functions by deploying them into software packages, assemble and chain them whenever required to deliver chained services to IoT devices. The combination of SDN and NFV allows increasing the efficiency and capacity of smart micro-grid networks without radically making change at the hardware level. Expanding the micro-grids network capacity can be achieved using an orchestrator, which can add new services without interrupting existing one or upgrading the network with new devices. The orchestrator is the NFV management and network orchestration (MANO) tool, which is responsible for controlling and managing NFV compute, storage, and network resources.

Besides, SDN and Data analytics are needed for context-aware data processing, filtering, aggregation, and mining to capture the knowledge and generate high-level abstracted context information. It can also be used to react and trigger specific events to change the behavior of IoT devices, e.g. automating and adapting the indoor lighting, closing curtains, switching off the light, ensure the comfort level by controlling the HVAC equipment's, etc. SDN and Big Data analytics could also be used to offload some functions from sensors, i.e. by allowing the creation of software sensors inside mediation servers, etc. Therefore, first we need a powerful approach to allow smart devices understanding their own context and adapt themselves "on-the-fly" for optimal energy-efficiency and performance under all communication scenario. Second, we also need to bring the computation from cloud computing infrastructures the network edge in single hop proximity of IoT sensing devices to create micro data centers, i.e. cloudlets. Such cloudlets should support context semantics to achieve QoS prioritization among distributed HVAC sensors and/or actuators and differentiate the traffic exchanged among them. Third, we need a centralized management and configuration of the cloudlets infrastructure, orchestrate the communication in a flexible and agile manner.

In this paper, we introduce an intuitive system, less computation intensive, easy to implement on small modular low-cost Single Board Computer like Raspberry Pi, and amenable to online adaptation to the variations in ambient temperature, solar heat input through windows etc. In the context of our energy-efficiency management system in micro data center, we make the following contributions in this paper:

- We present a novel IoT network virtualization approach based on SDN/NFV to offer a high degree of automation in service chaining delivery for IoT devices. Our solution enables offloading expensive computation at the network edge and offers a high degree of automation in service chaining delivery for IoT devices.

- We introduce an IoT data model that provides a data collection facility to accommodate HVAC sensors and actuators, where data are generated and consumed locally in smart campus buildings.
- We describe a novel Context-Awareness Model to represent the functional intelligence that identifies a set of contexts, transition rules, dependencies, and relations between contexts, to control energy appliances in smart buildings.
- We provide a novel approach to realize context information enhanced with Time Series Data Repository (TSDR) approach to model hierarchical structures and relationships for collecting, storing, querying, and maintaining time series data in the SDN controller.
- We present a prototype implementation to show the proposed architecture framework can be deployed in both educational and residential smart campus buildings using low-cost hardware and lightweight Docker virtualization.

The remainder of this paper is organized as follows: Sect. 2 describes the related work on context-aware energy management IoT systems and highlights the use of SDN for context IoT data delivery. Section 3 devolves into the proposed architecture, which integrates our context-aware algorithm into a SDN infrastructure to realize efficient energy management in the network edge. Section 4 presents the details of a proof-of-concept implementation along with two use case which will benefit from the proposed architecture. Section 5 presents concluding remarks alluding to lessons learned and future work.

2   Related Work

This section describes the related work on context aware sensing towards an efficient energy management systems and highlights the researches promoting SDN for programmable provision of context aware data delivery.

2.1   Context-Aware Sensing in Smart Buildings

Service oriented middleware such as has been introduced for integrating heterogeneous IoT domain context data into a unified context broker. For example, COLLECT [20] receives contextual complex events, performs reasoning with context rules, and provides advises about the actions to take on the detected event patterns. A context aware sensing approach for efficient energy communication in IoT is described in [24] to allow IoT devices learning contextual information, e.g. channel conditions, QoS demand, battery condition, etc. from their own experience and adapt themselves "on-the-fly" for optimal energy efficiency. Additionally, a semantic reasoning system based on Semantic Web technologies was proposed [6, 15] to facilitate interoperability among diverse IoT applications operating in a realistic context-aware environment. Likewise, [17] introduced a Semantic Web server for logging temperature values and store the gathered raw data in a time-series database.

The CAEMS framework [13] uses an off-line ontology model for sharing the context knowledge on behalf of the energy consumption, and predict the expected future context information based on the historical data values. Venkatesh et al. [29] introduced an ontology-based context engine to reduce the compute redundancy and computational complexity of the IoT distributed infrastructure. A middleware layer is used to translate low-level heterogeneous data gathered from wearable computing sensors, e.g. GPS location, blood pressure, heartbeat, etc. to a single higher-level abstracted context. The ContQuest [21] service oriented middleware uses an ontology-based context reasoning agent captures the context-related characteristics and maps these resources into a uniform description model. Narendra et al. [18] proposed a goal-driven context-aware data filtering algorithm was aligned with the semantic sensor network ontology.

Nonetheless, Semantic Web technologies is strongly coupled with applications and its expressive power does not allow advanced capabilities to express the logical and semantic reasoning context. Ontology representation is resource intensive and can be complex to perform information retrieval. Moreover, data need to be modeled in a compatible format (e.g. OWL, RDF), which limits its performance and numerical reasoning. Our approach used key-value modeling to facilitate data retrieval from Big Data store and introduced a transformation model for collecting, storing, querying, and maintaining context-aware data in the SDN controller.

2.2 SDN for Context Data Delivery

SDN has been used a context-aware network service layer to enable self-adaptation of virtual network function deployment [16]. The authors in [27] enhanced the SDN controller to create contextual overlay network graphs and monitors the network links and nodes as well as performing data analytics and edge processing and storage. They also introduced soft sensors [28] to obtain spatial and temporal distribution of content requests to perform optimal content placement in the cloud for mobile users. Similarly, Haw et al. [8] proposed a context-aware content delivery scheme that combines SDN and Content Centric Networking (CCN) to improve content delivery in mobile cloud networks. Luc et al. [14] introduced a context-aware traffic forwarding service to create a composition scheme between the SDN controller and the upper network applications while providing an abstracted forwarding functions for the lower layer.

Likewise, Du et al. [3] extended the OpenFlow model to IoT gateways at the network edge to attach contextual information, e.g. geo-localization data from GPS sensors and wearable devices, to OpenFlow packet header. Kathiravelu et al. [10] introduced the Cassowary middleware based on AMQP as a northbound binding to integrate sensing devices into the SDN network seamlessly. An AMQP broker extracts features available from sensing devices such as motion, temperature or humidity detection and uses a context awareness reasoning model to filter and process the collected raw data. Nova et al. [19] introduced the Capillary Network Platform for interconnecting and virtualizing IoT devices over the cellular backbone.

Despite the promise, these contributions lack of a precise context reasoning model since the context is not well-defined or vaguely introduced. Our approach provides an efficient data aggregation and data query to enabled centralized topology view that can be leveraged by multiple data-driven IoT applications. It used SDN northbound interface to query data from data store, and leverages Grafana to visualize the collected data.

Moreover, it provides NetFlow data retrieving to collect SDN Flow data and logging from the underlying network elements in the micro data center in the edge domain.

3   Design and Implementation of the Proposed Solution

This section presents the architectural details of our proposed solution to realize our SDN-enabled efficient energy management system.

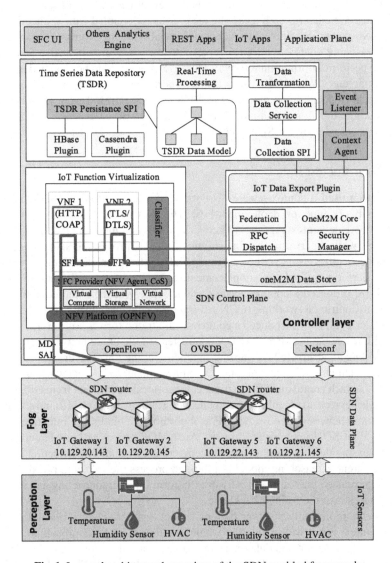

Fig. 1. Layered architectural overview of the SDN-enabled framework

3.1   Architectural Overview

Figure 1 illustrates the architecture of our framework, which is composed of three layers: at the bottom, is the *perception layer*, which comprises the sensing layer and the aggregator. The sensing layer encompasses all smart IoT sensors, e.g. temperature, humidity, air quality sensors, and the HVAC actuators, which have direct connectivity to the network via short range PAN technologies such RF, Bluetooth, ZigBee, etc. Aggregator sinks collect data from sensing layer and act as bridges between sensor nodes and IoT gateways, which act as a network proxy with the rest of the network. IoT sensors and actuators use message queuing client (MQTT) for publishing and subscribing data to/from IoT gateways. For example, IoT sensors gather temperature readings periodically, listen to network events through MQTT protocol, and send commands to IoT gateways to control fans and HVAC system. These IoT devices use four MQTT messages to publish-subscribe data: i) *Connect* message allows client to connect to remote M2M broker inside IoT gateways. It trigger a callback function to handle any incoming MQTT messages on the subscribed topics; ii) *Send* message is used by sensors to publish data to IoT brokers and receive command data back to it; *Store* message allows MQTT traffic incoming to brokers to be stored in time series database for retrieval in the future, and iii) *Use* message allows using Restful API for client applications to make use of their stored data. Furthermore, these IoT devices make of three QoS levels (i.e. QoS 0, QoS 1, and QoS 2) to create different priority levels for the published data.

Next, we have the *fog layer*, which is located in single hop proximity of the IoT sensing devices and include all the network equipment to realize the micro-grid communication infrastructure. It consists of IoT gateways (shown in Fig. 2) that interface with the perception layer to receive raw data from the sensors, and send commands to control the actuators. The gateway concept is prevalent in home ADSL models and WiFi access points. The design of IoT gateway is different since it should be able to integrate heterogeneous smart objects and expose their resources and make them available to the rest of IoT network. Additionally, IoT gateways are connected to the SDN network through SDN routers (i.e. virtual and physical), which embed an OpenFlow agent that has the capabilities to add, remove, update, and delete packets inside these routing devices.

The SDN routers (OpenVSwitch virtual routers in Fig. 2) are connected to a *SDN control layer* as shown in Fig. 1, i.e. the SDN controller, which embeds all the intelligence and maintains the network-wide view of the data path elements and links that connect them. The controller contains several modules we develop to integrate to the smart micro-grid network. First, the *IoT function virtualization module* (will be described in Sect. 3.3), which expands the micro-grids network capacity by deploying virtualized IoT functions into software packages that can be assembled and chained whenever required to deliver chained services to IoT devices. Thanks to NFV platform (e.g. OPNFV in Fig. 1) that encompasses an orchestrator (i.e. SFC provider) which can add new services without interrupting existing one or upgrading the network with new devices. The orchestrator is the NFV management and network orchestration (MANO) tool, which is responsible for controlling and managing NFV compute, storage, and network resources.

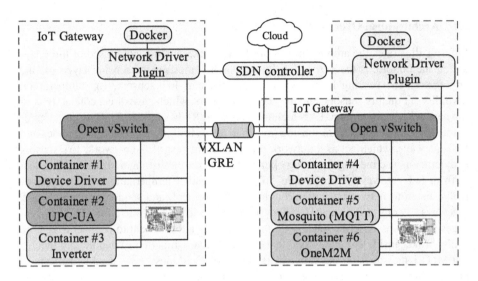

Fig. 2. IoT gateways

Second, the SDN control layer contains the IoT management model to perform communication with IoT sensors through IoT data management and service capability's module i.e. *IoT Data Export Plugin* (will be described in Sect. 3.2) for accomplishing M2M operations at scale. It also includes a *context agent* (will be discussed in Sect. 3.4) embeds the context-aware model to perform context reasoning needed for data processing, filtering, and aggregation, and to capture the knowledge and generate high-level abstracted context information. Third, the controller layer comprises a data processing module that make use of a Time Series Data Repository (TSDR) module to perform real-time data processing and analytics, data transformation and collection services: upon received at the data store, the IoT Data Export Plugin triggers CRUD handling operations to enable writing data in the data-store before connecting them to the context-aware middleware to perform data processing. The TSDR module connects to Cassandra and HBase NoSQL database management system through plugins.

3.2 IoT Data Management Model

The IoT data management model is based on a data-centric IoT message broker that make use of standardized oneM2M API to allow authorized sensors and applications retrieving the data stored by other devices. In particular, the model implements a hierarchical containment tree where each node in the tree represents an IoT resource. As depicted in Fig. 3, the tree contains different data and measurements of IoT devices and their associated attributes. Each node in the tree represents a specific resource an IoT device can interact with using either the Message Queuing Telemetry Transport (MQTT) broker or direct HTTP-like message exchange. Those attributes provide resources description in a form of meta-data that includes information about the resource creation, access rights, creator of the resource, content size, creation time and date, etc.

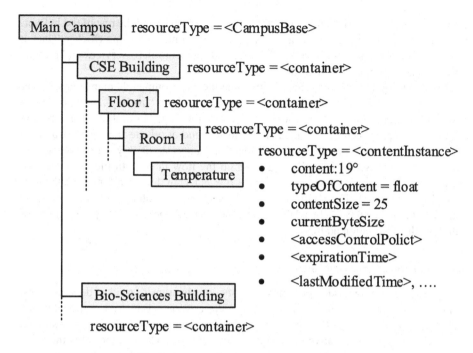

Fig. 3. Resources tree comprising IoT data.

As shown in Fig. 1, the oneM2M Data Store represents the back-end database where raw sensor data are stored. The proposed architecture supports CRUDN (create, retrieve, update, delete, and notify) operations for collecting sensing data from remote IoT sensors. Such an approach allows us to easily perform inventory with life-cycle management of IoT devices and perform big data analytics on raw sensor's data, retrieve and transform them into appropriate context representation.

3.3   IoT Service Chaining

In Fig. 1, the *IoT Function Virtualization (IoT NFV)* module shows our proposal for mapping IoT sensors into virtualized functions that follows the ETSI guideline for NFV architectural framework. The SDN controller is merged with the IoT management platform (i.e. NFV Platform) to perform communication between IoT gateways and their remote sensors and enforce the security of state information. The IoT-NFV module uses lightweight containers to enable the creation of multiple isolated virtual IoT gateways inside a single physical one. For example, VNF1 and VNF2 in Fig. 1 represent two independent virtualized functions chained to form a single IoT service. Constrained Application Protocol (CoAP) messages in VNF1 coming from sensors in the sensing layer are chained with DTLS service to enforce the security of IoT resources. Similarly, other group of sensors in the sensing layer that make use of HTTP/REST services in VNF1 can see their messages chained and secured with TLS in VNF2 to optimize the cooperation between IoT devices, intermediate infrastructure and the rest of the IoT network. The virtualization layer is based on lightweight containers using Docker. Thus, it becomes fast to create, install, run and deploy independent micro-services and provide simple service composition facilities.

Routing the packets among these VNF components is completely managed and controlled by the SDN controller. Thanks to Pipework and the "overlay" mode of OpenVSwitch software router. The former allows connecting together multiple containers in arbitrarily complex scenarios. The later provides a kind of private IP addresses that are only valid internally. Each IP address P identifies a service deployment in a separate chain, so that the SDN controller can program the flow table with the required flow entries F_P to define the following component $B = F_P(A)$ in the chain for which the traffic will be forwarded. The controller creates for each flow entry F_P the forward table entries that matches received packets against the forwarding ports A they should follow with P as the destination address.

3.4   Context-Awareness Model

The context reasoning model identifies a set of contexts, transition rules, dependencies, and relations between contexts. Figure 4 illustrates the context-awareness model which includes a 3-tuple (A_k, T_k, D_k), Where is A_k is the action knowledge, T_k is Transitional knowledge, and D_k declarative knowledge. The action knowledge represents the functional intelligence for a given environment, which is coded using logic rules or machine learning algorithm. For example, given a current temperature inside a room, the system should switch on or off HVAC system of the building.

The transition knowledge specifies when a passage to another context should be performed. It can be expressed for example as IF(conditions) then(activation) transition rules, fuzzy rules or neural network probability condition. Finally, the declarative knowledge provides description of some aspects of the context to include some pre-acquired knowledge for the context. For example, number of invited guest in convocation hall, room size, room usage schedule, etc.

The context reasoning model is used to subdivide the knowledge into multi-level hierarchy, each level is used to represent vertical relationship between sub-levels. Figure 5 illustrates an example context hierarchy for an educational building. The vertical multi-level hierarchy describes the relationship between groups in a given set $G = \{G_1, G_2, ..., G_n\}$, where a given group $G_i \in G$ contains a set of mutually exclusive contexts $C_i = C_0^i, ..., C_a^i, ..., C_n^i$. An active context C_a^i in a subset of group G_i is active within the context of its parents. That is, to make the inheritance active, transitional and declarative knowledge from selected contexts in groups that are hierarchically above G_i.

In our case, Fig. 5 illustrates the reasoning model where Campus buildings are the first group G_1. The second group G_2, we identify different types of buildings, e.g. educational, residential, administrative, laboratory buildings, etc. To apply this context-aware reasoning model to our case, we should activate the set of contexts that best suits to a given situation. The active context will control all the execution process, define behaviors of our actuators, specify the constraints and all other context-dependent characteristics. For seek of simplicity, we define an example of our context reasoning model from Fig. 5 as follows:

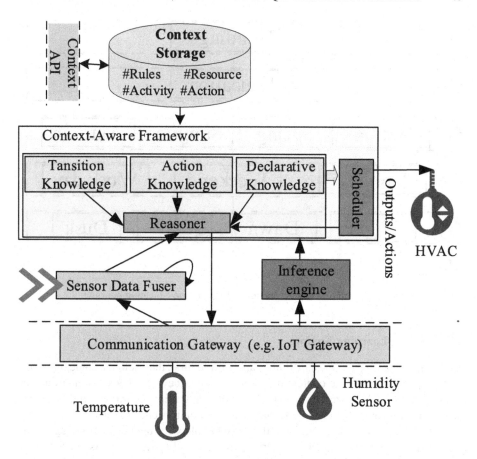

Fig. 4. Context-awareness model

- C^t_{Active} = {Buildings, Educational, Spring, Working-Day, Day}.
- C^{t+1}_{Active} = {Buildings, Residential, Spring, Working-Day, Night}.
- C^{t+2}_{Active} = {Buildings, Educational, Winter, Holiday, Day}.

Specifically, given active contexts C^t_{Active} and C^{t+1}_{Active} at certain instances t and $t+1$, it might be seen easy or even not much complicated to identify the process to manage context operation, in particular given the slow evolution of sensor variables such as temperature, humidity and CO2 level inside rooms in education buildings. However, given different situation that occur in a given group G_i, we identify a domain of services s_i which has its own execution thread(s) and its control is a function of context C^t_{Active}. The control of service s_i can be defined by Eq. 1:

$$\text{Control of } s_i = \Gamma(C^t_{Active}) \qquad (1)$$

Where Γ is the context reasoning framework operating within s_i. For example, room temperature behave differently if a door/window is open/closed or if the room is empty or occupied, electrical lights and fans behave accordingly to these situations.

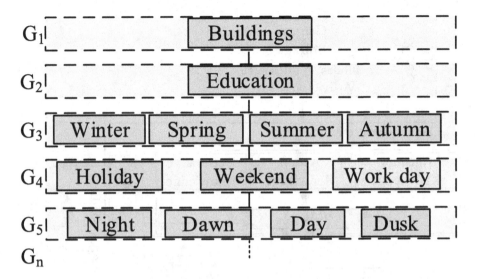

Fig. 5. Example of context hierarchy levels for an education building

3.5 Machine Learning Engine

The machine learning engine capabilities are twofold: first, they help the context reasoning framework to infer the context decisions. Second, they feed back the environment changes to the SDN controller to perform automatic traffic steering and policy placement. For the former, the machine learning engine monitors current sensor's data delivery and predicts future data and learn the optimal policy for the network management. In particular, the energy demand is variable in time and space, since its consumption varies qualitatively and quantitatively on the time of days, e.g. working days, holidays, week-end, etc. or the location where IoT devices are deployed, e.g. laboratories, classrooms, office building, etc. The machine learning engine provides better personalized experience and give priorities to specific IoT devices that should communicate relevant information to the SDN controller. It also enables storing and processing the collected data to analyze the data-sets based on certain parameters such as location, time, and historical data.

For the later, Fig. 6 depicts the machine learning module where the SDN controller continuously learns from data generated by virtual routers and becomes aware of the runtime status of the network. The controller collects OpenFlow statistics (circle 1), applies ML algorithm i.e. multi-layer perceptron (circle 2), and take the right decisions that adjust the policies (i.e. traffic flow redirection from $A \Rightarrow D$ to $A \Rightarrow B \Rightarrow D$ or $A \Rightarrow C \Rightarrow D$) for traffic classification and traffic shaping, dynamically change these policies according to the analytics results, and feed back these results to the forwarding path for automatic steering and policy placement. The controller can also use the machine learning capabilities to establish normalized profiles to predict traffic pattern, and perform routing optimization based on predetermined or dynamically update learned rules.

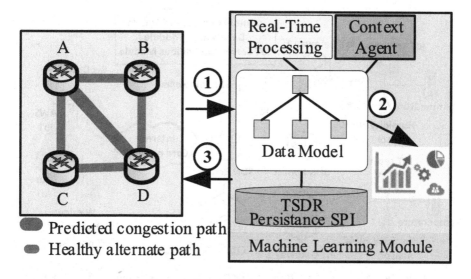

Fig. 6. Traffic congestion prediction with automated control.

4 Proof of Concept Implementation

This section describes the primary prototype implementation we realized to verify the feasibility of running the platform. We first introduce the platform implementation, then we highlight two application test cases.

4.1 Platform

Figure 7 depicts our target application. IoT gateways are based on a single-board computer Raspberry Pi 3 with 1 GB of memory and a quad-core ARMv8 BCM2837B0 Cortex-A53 ARM Cortex-A53 CPU running at 1.2 GHz. The gateway connects to the network using its integrated 2.4 GHz 802.11n interface. It also contains *hostapd* user space daemon software we used to create virtual wireless networks inside the same physical one. IoT gateways are equipped with 40 pins GPIO interfaces to connect to wide range of sensors and actuators.

We deployed several sensor boards that act as Cluster Head (CH) nodes to collect raw sensor data and measure the surrounding air quality from all Cluster Members (CM). CMs sensor nodes periodically measures temperature, humidity and Co2 levels, compare them with the last measurement, if results had changed, they send an advertisement message (ADV) to the cluster head. Examples of CMs we used include *DHT22* temperature and humidity sensors; the *MQ-135* Co2-Gas sensor; and the *K30 CO2* module that gathers the level of oxygen inside our campus buildings and student housing residence. We also used smart energy meter to detect and report power consumption to CH nodes and IoT gateways. As Cluster Heads (CH) we used multiple NodeMCU IoT platforms running on-top of the ESP8266 Wi-Fi SoC, which also integrate a TCP/IP protocol stack that allows access to our virtual Wi-Fi network running on IoT gateways.

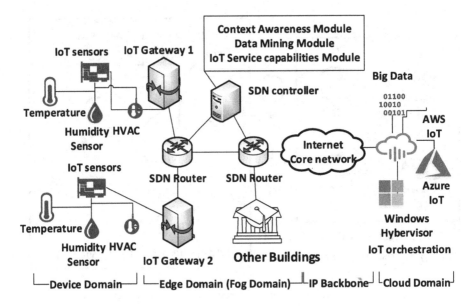

Fig. 7. Network topology used as the target application

We successfully connected these CHs through the MQTT broker running on IoT gateways. We used also CoAP API to connect some other sensors to ESP8266 board. COAP servers are deployed inside IoT gateways in a form of lightweight containers.

Additionally, our SDN controller is based on the OpenDaylight (ODL) Project, which has several SDN and application management capabilities. The ODL platform can be configured to run as a highly scaled up and out distributed cluster with IoT, SDN and NFV functions. It can also be integrated with OpenStack and deployed to communicate with a high traffic data center. We used OpenVSwitch (OVS) as our distributed virtual multi-layer SDN switch managed by our SDN controller. We used two OVS modes: NAT and bridge. The NAT mode is used to connect the SDN routers with outside world. The OVS bridge mode offers virtual interfaces we used to connect with docker instances to multi-host networking, i.e. we used both internal IP addresses as our pseudo-IP and MAC addresses.

4.2 Service Function Chain Composition in Education Building

For the education buildings, we consider diverse CH nodes in charge of collecting temperature, humidity levels and CO2 concentration from CM sensors of occupied indoor spaces. We consider three VNFs implemented inside docker images: $Tensor_{VNF}$, $Mosquitto_{VNF}$, and $OneM2M_{VNF}$ as described in Fig. 8. The first VNF monitors the current sensor's data delivery, uses TensorFlow machine learning models to predict future data from correlated sensor's readings, and learn the optimal policy for the network management by avoiding redundant readings. The second VNF gathers sensors readings periodically, listen to network events through MQTT protocol, and send commands to control fans and HVAC system. Finally, the third VNF establish the access to IoT resources through the hierarchical containment tree described in Sect. 3.2.

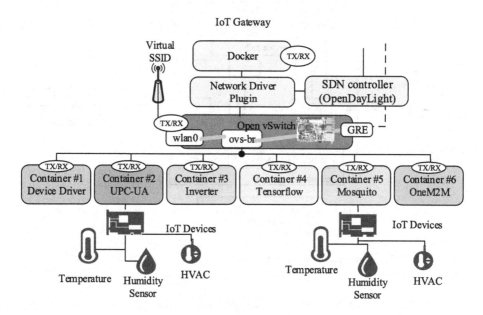

Fig. 8. Network topology used as the target application.

In order to interconnect different micro-services running in containers, we used Docker engine v19.03. Docker engine offers advanced network capabilities to manage connectivity between containers. As shown in Fig. 8, we used Docker Network Driver Plugin to create virtual docker network that connects to virtual SDN routers (Open-VSwitch) and handles all coordination between virtual hosts. We also configured persistent docker volume to store alarms and other debugging events outside docker containers. We also used Vagrant for automating the creation of virtual machine instances, building and maintaining portable virtual Docker containers.

We deployed Docker swarm as our container's orchestration tool to manage different VNFs we deployed in our tests. Docker swarm offers a high level of availability for the running application. We defined one of our containers as a leader to manage membership and delegation among the other containers, which we configured as workers. It is worth noting that we can use Kubernetes (K3s) system for automating deployment, scaling, and management of VNFs. We configured Docker Swarm to use docker-compose configuration files and scripts we created to tell the docker daemon (running inside each IoT gateway) how to pull the appropriate container image from the Docker Hub repository, how to establish networking between VNFs, how to mount storage volumes, and where to store logs for a given container.

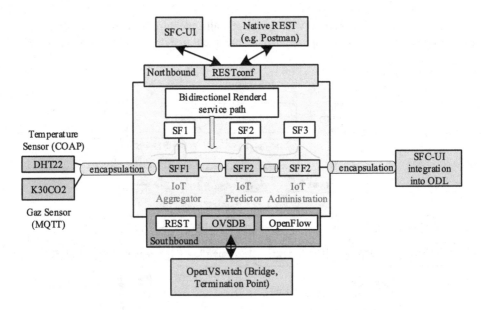

Fig. 9. SFC composition for Temperature and CO2 measurements as an IoT service.

Figure 9 describes the approach we used to configure the OpenDaylight SDN controller Service Function Chaining (SFC) to define an ordered list of network services (i.e. $Tensor_{VNF}$, $Mosquitto_{VNF}$, and $OneM2M_{VNF}$) which we stitched together to create a service chain. This SFC is arranged as: i) physical network function (PNF) that contains the IoT temperature and gas sensors, ii) three IoT VNFs depicted as Service Function Forwarders (SFF) in Fig. 9, and iii) the SFC-UI integration into the SDN controller. When the IoT SF1 is updated with new sensor measurements, an update SFC composition is triggered by the docker swarm orchestrator to pull and install a new image (or migrate an existing one) for the required VNF ($Mosquitto_{VNF}$, $Tensor_{VNF}$, or $OneM2M_{VNF}$), respectively. Our implementation shows that our approach is able to create, instantiate and deploy new customized on-demand virtualized IoT services that gather, process, estimate and supervise the air conditioning inside campus buildings. Our approach successfully collects room temperature, send these values to IoT VNFs through IoT gateways, which forward them to the SDN controller to switch ON or OFF the HVAC appliances based on temperature and CO2 threshold. This result is very flexible and reconfigurable as it can instantiate and deploy VNFs as needed for the scalability and allows saving up to 70% of the energy consumption in the campus buildings.

4.3   Activity Management in Residential Building

Monitoring users activity in residential building is very critical to understand how they interact with IoT home appliances (e.g. TV boxes, PlayStation (PS), washing machine, Laptop, Lights, etc.) because different users activities usually call for different services.

Therefore, we add an Activity Recognition (AR) model to the context-awareness model described in Sect. 3.4.

Table 1. Daily occurring user activity in smart residential building

Activity	Sleep	Use Lap-top	Study in office	Watch TV	Read Book	Play PS	Prepare food	Washing clothes	No One at home
Occurrence %	33	10	8.3	12.5	6.8	7.1	9.2	4.3	8.8

The AR model describes the user behavior inside smart residential home as shown in Table 1. The AR model is trained using semi-supervised learning model (which is included in the ML engine in Fig. 10) to forecast the appliances a user is using during the activities describes in Table 1. For example, if a user activity is "*Sleep*", only night

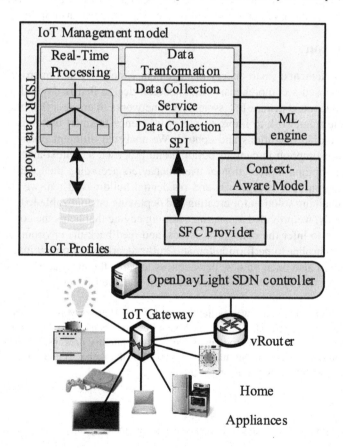

Fig. 10. Typical smart home network as an IoT service.

light of bedroom should be ON and all other appliances should be OFF. Similarly, if the weather is getting warmer, the HVAC or fans should be ON automatically; if no one at home all lights and appliances should be OFF.

Figure 10 depicts the IoT gateway, which can be easily turned into a virtual SDN router using OpenVSwitch and Docker Network Driver Plugin services. The SDN controller can manage the whole Home Area network. The controller monitors link states periodically via the link layer discovery protocol and creates the network topology. Additionally, the approach we develop in this paper allows slicing the Home Area network into several separated logical networks, each network partition can deal with different QoS requirements. For example, a network partition with strict QoS requirements can be configured for CCTV Camera and video streaming, etc. This result of architecture can successfully discover a lot of useful data from the AR model. It also success in creating several separated logical networks, which improve the network agility, availability and performance. Moreover, the proposed architecture performs energy saving by automatically switching ON/OFF unnecessary home appliances based on the context-awareness and AR models. The SDN controller collect useful data for context-aware service provisioning and manages the forwarding tables of SDN routers to provide comfort and assistance to building occupants, and apply powerful learning models on collected data to derive behaviors that impact high energy consumption.

5   Conclusion

In order to implement a smart energy management system in smart micro-grids, in this paper we proposed a comprehensive architectural design that is devised to empower SDN-enabled Context-Aware IoT systems and networks to create a flexible, agile, and reconfigurable framework to improve energy efficiency in smart buildings and enable automated building operations and control. We analyzed different parameters affecting energy consumption in campus building and proposed a context-awareness model that allows an optimum prediction of users behaviors according their daily consumed energy profiles in both educational and residential buildings. Then, we introduced a IoT service chaining solution for creating and deploying customizable IoT services on-demand. Finally, we provided a machine learning engine that helps the context reasoning framework to infer the context decisions, and feed back the environment changes to the SDN controller to perform automatic traffic steering and policy placement. The architecture will also open up new perspectives towards the mass adoption of efficient energy management systems based on robust and scalable IoT services.

Acknowledgments. This work was partially funded by the Tunisian Ministry of Higher Education and Scientific Research (MES) under the Young Researchers Incentive Program (19PEJC09-04) and the CV Raman research program 2017675. Any opinions, findings, and conclusions or recommendations expressed in this material are those of the author(s) and do not necessarily reflect the views of MES or CV Raman program.

References

1. European Environment Agency: Progress on energy efficiency in Europe (2019). https://bit.ly/2OygVJN

2. Alam, I., et al.: A survey of network virtualization techniques for internet of things using SDN and NFV. ACM Comput. Surv. **53**(2), 1–40 (2020)
3. Du, P., Putra, P., Yamamoto, S., Nakao, A.: A context-aware IoT architecture through software-defined data plane. In: 2016 IEEE Region 10 Symposium (TENSYMP), pp. 315–320 (2016)
4. Energy Information Administration (EIA): International energy outlook (2019). https://bit.ly/2CFN9QK
5. U.S. Department of Energy's: Increasing efficiency of building systems and technologies (2015). https://bit.ly/2CodZgd
6. Guner, A., Kurtel, K., Celikkan, U.: A message broker based architecture for context aware IoT application development. In: 2017 International Conference on Computer Science and Engineering (UBMK), pp. 233–238 (2017)
7. Hakiri, A., Gokhale, A., Berthou, P., Schmidt, D.C., Gayraud, T.: Software-defined networking: challenges and research opportunities for future internet. Comput. Netw. **75**, 453–471 (2014)
8. Haw, R., Alam, M.G.R., Hong, C.S.: A context-aware content delivery framework for QoS in mobile cloud. In: The 16th Asia-Pacific Network Operations and Management Symposium, pp. 1–6 (2014)
9. Hirsch, A., Parag, Y., Guerrero, J.: Microgrids: a review of technologies, key drivers, and outstanding issues. Renew. Sustain. Energy Rev. **90**, 402–411 (2018)
10. Kathiravelu, P., Sharifi, L., Veiga, L.: Cassowary: middleware platform for context-aware smart buildings with software-defined sensor networks. In: Proceedings of the 2nd Workshop on Middleware for Context-Aware Applications in the IoT, M4IoT 2015, pp. 1–6 (2015)
11. Kreutz, D., Ramos, F.M.V., Veríssimo, P.E., Rothenberg, C.E., Azodolmolky, S., Uhlig, S.: Software-defined networking: a comprehensive survey. Proc. IEEE **103**(1), 14–76 (2015). https://doi.org/10.1109/JPROC.2014.2371999
12. Kumar, S., Islam, S., Jolfaei, A.: Microgrid communications - protocols and standards, pp. 291–326. Energy Engineering. Institution of Engineering and Technology (2019)
13. Kyselova, A.G., Verbitskyi, I.V., Kyselov, G.D.: Context-aware framework for energy management system. In: 2nd International Conference on Intelligent Energy and Power Systems (IEPS), pp. 1–4 (2016)
14. Luo, S., Wu, J., Li, J., Guo, L., Pei, B.: Context-aware traffic forwarding service for applications in SDN. In: IEEE International Conference on Smart City SocialCom SustainCom (SmartCity), pp. 557–561 (2015)
15. Maarala, A.I., Su, X., Riekki, J.: Semantic reasoning for context-aware Internet of Things applications. IEEE Internet Things J. **4**(2), 461–473 (2017)
16. Martini, B., Paganelli, F., Mohammed, A.A., Gharbaoui, M., Sgambelluri, A., Castoldi, P.: SDN controller for context-aware data delivery in dynamic service chaining. In: Proceedings of the 2015 1st IEEE Conference on Network Softwarization (NetSoft), pp. 1–5 (2015)
17. Najem, N., Haddou, D.B., Abid, M.R., Darhmaoui, H., Krami, N., Zytoune, O.: Context-aware wireless sensors for IoT-centeric energy-efficient campuses. In: 2017 IEEE International Conference on Smart Computing (SMARTCOMP), pp. 1–6 (2017)
18. Narendra, N., Ponnalagu, K., Ghose, A., Tamilselvam, S.: Goal-driven context-aware data filtering in IoT-based systems. In: 2015 IEEE 18th International Conference on Intelligent Transportation Systems, pp. 2172–2179 (2015)
19. Novo, O., Beijar, N., Ocak, M., Kjällman, J., Komu, M., Kauppinen, T.: Capillary networks - bridging the cellular and IoT worlds. In: 2015 IEEE 2nd World Forum on Internet of Things (WF-IoT), pp. 571–578 (2015)
20. de Prado, A.G., Ortiz, G., Boubeta-Puig, J.: COLLECT: COLLaborativE context-aware service oriented architecture for intelligent decision-making in the Internet of Things. Expert. Syst. Appl. **85**, 231–248 (2017)

21. Pötter, H.B., Sztajnberg, A.: Adapting heterogeneous devices into an IoT context-aware infrastructure. In: 2016 IEEE/ACM 11th International Symposium on Software Engineering for Adaptive and Self-Managing Systems (SEAMS), pp. 64–74 (2016)
22. Rashid, H., Mammen, P.M., Singh, S., Ramamritham, K., Singh, P., Shenoy, P.: Want to reduce energy consumption? Don't depend on the consumers! In: Proceedings of the 4th ACM International Conference on Systems for Energy-Efficient Built Environments (2017)
23. Sen, S.: Invited - context-aware energy-efficient communication for IoT sensor nodes. In: Proceedings of the 53rd Annual Design Automation Conference (2016)
24. Sen, S.: Invited: context-aware energy-efficient communication for IoT sensor nodes. In: 2016 53nd ACM/EDAC/IEEE Design Automation Conference (DAC), pp. 1–6 (2016)
25. Singh, S., Jha, R.K.: A survey on software defined networking: architecture for next generation network. J. Netw. Syst. Manag. **25**(2), 321–374 (2016)
26. Staddon, S.C., Cycil, C., Goulden, M., Leygue, C., Spence, A.: Intervening to change behaviour and save energy in the workplace: a systematic review of available evidence. Energy Res. Soc. Sci. **17**, 30–51 (2016)
27. Tosic, M., Ikovic, O., Boskovic, D.: SDN based service provisioning management in smart buildings. In: 39th International Convention on Information and Communication Technology, Electronics and Microelectronics (MIPRO), pp. 754–759 (2016)
28. Tosic, M., Ikovic, O., Boskovic, D.: Soft sensors in wireless networking as enablers for SDN based management of content delivery. In: 2016 39th International Convention on Information and Communication Technology, Electronics and Microelectronics (MIPRO), pp. 559–564 (2016)
29. Venkatesh, J., Chan, C., Akyurek, A.S., Rosing, T.S.: A modular approach to context-aware IoT applications. In: IEEE First International Conference on Internet-of-Things Design and Implementation (IoTDI), pp. 235–240 (2016)
30. Zhang, T.: NFV Platform Design: A Survey. arXiv: 2002.11059v2 (2020)
31. Zhu, Y., Wang, F., Yan, J.: The potential of distributed energy resources in building sustainable campus: the case of Sichuan University. Energy Procedia **145**, 582–585 (2018)

Quality of Experience Aware Replication Framework for Video Streaming in Content-Centric Mobile Networks Based on SDN Architecture

Amna Fekih[1,3](✉) [iD], Sonia Gaied Fantar[2,3], and Habib Youssef[1,3]

[1] Computer Science Department, Higher Institute of Computer Science and Communication Techniques, University of Sousse, 4011 Hammam Sousse, Tunisia
emna.fekih@isetso.rnu.tn
[2] Computer Science Department, Higher School of Sciences and Technologies, University of Sousse, 4011 Hammam Sousse, Tunisia
[3] PRINCE Research Laboratory, University of Sousse, 4011 Hammam Sousse, Tunisia

Abstract. Despite the diversity and the high quantity of content exchanged on the Internet architecture, service providers want to offer the most efficient delivery content system in order to maximize customer satisfaction and subsequently increase their financial gain. Video streaming is the most popular way for all kind of multimedia content. In particular, the main objective of adaptive video streaming is to ensure user satisfaction while maximizing the use of resources.

Video streaming with all its characteristics and the constraints associated with the current Internet infrastructure emphasizes that the latter is inadequate to support video streaming, particularly with the continued growth of its various operations. For this reason, Content-Centric Networks (CCN) - the most popular ICN architecture - is an innovative solution proposed to eliminate host-communication-based Internet by adopting a content-centric approach. Although this solution is promising, the huge overhead costs resulting from the CCN forwarding process without forgetting the size of the CCN forwarding table that swells more and more with the network size and the exchanged content quantity requires a deep revision of CCN's efficiency and adaptability for large-scale networks. In this context, we present a new replication framework for video streaming in Content-Centric Mobile Networks based on SDN Architecture (RF-VS-SD-CCMN) to achieve better content delivery, improve the quality perceived by users (QoE), and enhance the consumption of network resources. The experiments, that were carried out with the ndnSIM simulator, have clearly shown the efficiency of our solution.

Keywords: SDN · CCN · Video streaming · In-network caching · Monitoring

1 Introduction

Over the past decades, video streaming has put a huge strain on the underlying distribution network. With this exponential emergence, the Internet is applying incremental

© Springer Nature Switzerland AG 2020
I. Jemili and M. Mosbah (Eds.): DiCES-N 2020, CCIS 1348, pp. 75–94, 2020.
https://doi.org/10.1007/978-3-030-65810-6_5

patches over time to be able to support and manage new technological requirements, but its initial design is slowing it down. In other words, the network model is unchanged while the services that use the Internet have radically changed. These shortcomings have motivated the researchers to propose alternative architectures. Information-Centric Networks [1, 2] is based on a future architecture that processes any type of information requested regardless of where and how it is retrieved. Because of the braking consequences of the strong dependence between the content name and its location used by current Internet, CCN as a future architecture solution defines a naming scheme totally decoupled from location, content-based (re) routing and caching mechanisms to efficiently use network resources and properly support information that occurs continuously. CCN [2] is the most popular ICN. It has also recently been considered a promising architecture for Content-Centric Mobile Networks (CCMN) due to two main features such as named-based routing and in-network caching. However, CCMN is characterized by challenging features: user mobility, bandwidth overload, limitation of energy and especially slow and intermittent connectivity. So, default CCN is not suitable for MN domains directly. Therefore, providing a specific routing and caching policies to intermediate nodes is a priority task.

The majority of media traffic comes from streaming services like Netflix, YouTube. HTTP Adaptive Streaming (HAS) technologies which allow scalable distribution of video by shifting the rate adaptation to the user present the basis for these services already mentioned. Basically, the video is temporarily split into (pieces) chunks and encoded at different quality rates. Therefore, in the event of rate fluctuations the user is able to switch to a lower quality representation transparently based on buffer fill levels, device characteristics and network statistics. HAS is based on Advanced Video Coding (AVC). However, the latter creates some redundancy since each quality layer is independent of the others. To solve this problem and improve the quality, the scalable video coding (SVC) [3] can be used since it considers a basic quality layer to which any enhancement layer is added.

The infinite progress of video streaming complicates the management of the Internet architecture. This is mainly due to the strong coupling between the logic of control and forwarding in network equipment. In [4–9], the authors aim to break this coupling and define programmable, scalable, and open networks by defining transfer and control APIs. Software-Defined Networks - the fruit of these works - is characterized by a total separation between the forwarding and control planes, an easy network programmability, a support for existing applications and architectures and even for the deployment of new architectures with an open exchange.

The deployment of each of the technologies already mentioned can be explained by particular advantages. So, their combination offers additional benefits. By combining HAS with SVC, it improves cache hit ratio [11], minimizes load on servers [10], decreases cache redundancy [12], and overcomes the cache size constraint in CCN [16].

In CCN, multiple caches are capable of delivering requested content with different throughputs, making the task of throughput evaluation difficult. This can also cause video freezes with a dramatic increase in the number of quality switches. A gradual upgrade with SVC leads to more efficient quality switching [14]. Specifically in CCN, a user can use one or more caches during playback. CCN approach requires a clean slate of the current architecture. It, therefore, creates an incompatibility with traditional networks and makes deployment more difficult. SDN presents the ideal solution to implement and deploy this promising approach that offers a complete separation between the control and data planes and network programmability.

In previous work, we introduced and tested a replication management framework (SD-RF) for Content-Centric Networks based on SDN Architecture [23]. SD-RF is based on an SD-CCN architecture that combines the advantages of SDN such as flexibility, network programmability, and separation between control and data planes, and those of CCN such as in-network caching and mobility. Based on this architecture, we proposed this framework for storage placement and replica assignment following both off-line and on-line approaches. Our objectives were to minimize the content access latency from users, to maximize the traffic volume served by the replicas, and thus minimizing overall traffic cost and traffic load. In [24], we first investigated the caching and security aspects and we proposed a Secure In-network Caching Scheme (SICS) for CCN networks based on SDN architecture taking advantage of its global vision. To ensure the robustness of this architecture and to predict CCN node overloads or CCN node failure, we have proposed a proactive caching strategy learning based cooperative caching for CCN networks based SDN architecture [25]. This strategy is consolidated by a reassignment module to reassign a router according to network constraints continuously checked.

SD-RF is a solution that takes advantage of the strengths of SDN such as separation between control and data planes and flexibility, and those of CCN such as caching and mobility by integrating the CCN and SDN architectures. We propose new solutions both offline and online for storage placement and replica allocation based on this hybrid architecture to minimize content latency in user side, reduce the network load and consequently the traffic cost since the users are pushed to perfectly use the contents cached in the closest node. In [24], we first studied the caching and security aspects and we proposed a caching system for CCN networks exploiting the monitoring capability of SDN controllers. To ensure the robustness of this architecture and to predict CCN node overloads or CCN node failure, we have introduced a new proactive cooperative caching strategy that allows reassignment of a CCN node according to network constraints that are continuously checked [25].

In this paper, we detail a new replication framework in Content-Centric Networks based on SDN Architecture for video streaming applications (RF-VS-SD-CCN). The contributions of this work are threefold:

- We augment the CCN node with proactive features. The main improved functionalities of CCN nodes are traffic shaping, anticipation of interests, cooperative caching the users are pushed to perfectly use the contents cached in the closest node and content replication according to utility (cost delivery).
- We build the "family" concept defined by the joint analysis of user preferences similarity and mobility similarity that can help improve routing performance and cache hit ratio.
- We propose a new replication framework for video streaming in Content-Centric Mobile Networks based on SDN Architecture (RF-VS-SD-CCMN) to enhance the content delivery, the quality perceived by users (QoE), and the consumption of network resources.

The rest of this article is presented as follows. The state of the art is described in Sect. 2. Section 3 focuses on caching in CCN, Scalable Video Coding for DASH, and SD-CCN architecture for DASH. The RF-VS-SD–CCMN architecture and its operating principle is detailed in Sect. 4. Experiments and results analysis are detailed in Sect. 5. Finally, Sect. 6 concludes the paper.

2 Related Work

Emerging streaming technologies such as Adobe's HTTP Dynamic Streaming send the same video content with multiple resolutions to different consumers. Although users may experience frequent freezes if the bandwidth is not large enough to support video resolutions, SVC is characterized by automatically adapting to link fluctuations. In [11], the authors enumerated the advantages of SVC if it is applied to caching and uplink bandwidth. In [15], the authors propose to group the HAS sessions in unicast and to share the same content in a single multicast session for a better use of resources in 3GPP networks. Andelin et al. [16] propose a SVC-specific quality selection heuristic to take into account more specific algorithmic decisions (Fig. 1).

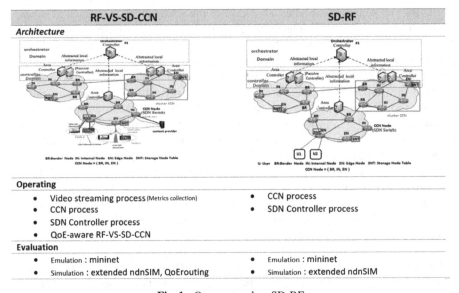

Fig. 1. Our proposal vs SD-RF

Lederer et al. present an architecture for DASH on CCN [13]. The authors identified several challenges primarily the transparent forwarding between multiple interfaces supported by name-based routing in ICN. [14] proposes an algorithm for scheduling video segment requests (DASH) in advance in order to improve the QoE of streaming video in ICN. An analysis of the influence of CCN caching under different time scales is detailed in [17] where the authors reported that with a cache of 10 GB and 1 TB, an average cache hit rate of approximately 25% and 45% respectively is achieved. Wenjie Li et al. [26] proposed a cache placement scheme to improve user QoE through cache partitioning. Measurements show that the proposed scheme can significantly reduce bit rate oscillation. However, these solutions do not take into account the constraints of cache size and scalability.

Other proposals have considered SDN as an ideal architecture to improve rate adaptation and subsequently improve the performance of video streaming applications. In [18], the authors implemented the adaptation logic by associating an adaptation device with the SDN controller and imposing a calculated bitrate to client. In [19], the selection of video quality is managed by a video control plan administered by an SDN controller. In [20], network congestion control is given to the SDN controllers in order to ensure reliable network service for real-time interactive applications. Nevertheless, these solutions do not consider in-network caching.

Alternatively, OpenCache [21] is the first proposed solution in the literature to provide network caching through an optimized SDN architecture. [22] proposed a new hybrid architecture based on the combination of SDN and CCN to provide assisted DASH-aware networking. The first solution [21] corresponds to our proposal in terms of control support of CCN nodes which ensured by the SDN controllers as well as the caching. Otherwise, our approach is built around CCN routers which are themselves classified, characterized natively by network distributed caching, and managed by one or more SDN controllers instead of defining new nodes to support caching. The second solution [22] has several points of intersection with our approach but clearly differs in terms of collecting statistics and classifying requests. Table 1 presents a summary of this related work. We compare these approaches cited as well as our proposal according to the characteristics considered.

3 Background

3.1 Caching in CCN

The main idea of CCN is to replace IP packets exchanged on the network by named content pieces. This architecture aims to re-modulate the Internet protocol stack in order to optimize the resources usage. The IP layer is replaced by the named data layer. Moreover, it is framed by two new layers. Below the strategy layer to minimize the demands on layer 2 and above the security layer which allows to secure the content itself rather than the connections in IP. In-network caching is considered an attractive feature of CCN because it can alleviate server bottleneck, reduce network traffic, and improve QoE. In CCN, by naming information in the network layer, each packet can be cached and retrieved easily because the network elements are aware of the information forwarded in the packets.

In CCN, each content router first consults its content store whenever it receives a interest packet and caches all of the information objects carried by the data packets. Path caching is therefore natively supported. However, off-path caching is not transparent to CCN as it first requires name configurations of the copies, then publishing them through the routing protocol, and updating the FIB tables to take into account these newly associated caches.

Table 1. Summary of related work

Paper	SDN	SDN model	CCN	Caching	Replication	VS
Idash [11]2011	×	-	×	×	×	√
Dash over CCN [13]2014	×	-	√	√	×	√
Congestion-aware edge caching [14]2015	×	-	√	√	×	√
Parallel adaptive http [15]2011	×	-	×	×	×	√
Quality selection for Dash [16]2012	×	-	×	×	×	√
CCN [17]2009	×	-	√	√	×	×
Delivering stable high-quality video [18] 2016	√	C	×	×	×	√
VCP [19] 2016	√	C	×	×	×	√
Congestion control for interactive applications [20] 2018	√	D	×	×	×	√
Ripplecache [26]2018	×	×	√	√	√	√
OpenCache [21] 2015	√	C	×	√	×	√
SD-RF [23] 2020	√	D	√	√	√	×
SICS [24] 2018	√	D	√	√	√	×
LECC [25] 2018	√	D	√	√	√	×
SDN-CCN-DASH[22] 2019	√	C	√	√	×	√
Our proposal	√	D	√	√	√	√

VS: Video Streaming processed   C: Centralized   D: Distributed

3.2   Scalable Video Coding for DASH

Since Dynamic adaptive streaming over HTTP (DASH) does not define a standardized technique for adapting video quality to network bandwidth, there are many ways to adapt the quality. In this article, we have used Dynamic Adaptive Streaming over HTTP (DASH) and Scalable Video Coding (SVC) to support video streaming over CCN.

Figure 2a shows a DASH system structure which consists of a DASH client which reads the content only after performing HTTP communications with an HTTP server. The latter encodes any video stream into several representations subsequently packaged in multimedia segments usually of the same duration. Caching is a primary key in video streaming systems to bring content close to end users and thereby reduce delay delivery and subsequently improve QoE.

Scalable Video Coding (SVC) [3] is a multi-layer codec that presents an extension of H264/AVC. Its particularity is the scalability. With SVC, each video is encoded in one base layer that provides minimum quality then this quality is progressively enhanced by adding the enhancement layers that offer different types of scalability such as spatial or temporal. Figure 2b shows the dependencies between layers. How each enhancement layer must be based on the base layer and the enhancement layer below it to can support the next higher level of video quality.

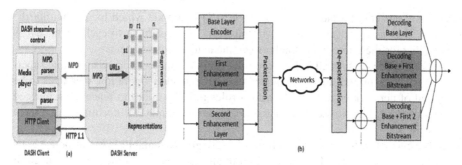

Fig. 2. (a) DASH system structure (b) Coding and decoding layers with Scalable Video Coding

3.3 SD-CCN Architecture for DASH

The CCN and MPEG DASH approaches share several common features. There are based on a customer-oriented model that initiates any request for desired content and also ensures distribution of customer content through multiple source support. A chunk is the base unit used by DASH as well as CCN that can be cached in the intermediate nodes along the delivery path. Therefore, the content delivery as well as packet loss recovery can be faster thanks to the caches scattered over the network.

On the other hand, the monitoring and management of DASH delivery via the controllers achieves high performance thanks to the information collected and exploited by SDN controllers to optimize content delivery and ensure scalability [31]. Table 2 summarizes the strengths and drawbacks of CCN and SDN architectures and also highlights the motivations and challenges for their integration.

4   Rf-VS-SD-CCN

4.1   RF-VS-SD-CCN Architecture

Our architecture is composed of a set of controllers deployed according to a topology defined by network operators for dynamic management of CCN clusters. The controllers are responsible for communicating with the orchestrator for the purpose of exchanging synchronization information and building their own network view periodically. In our architecture, a controller can be active or passive. It is active if at least one CCN node is attached. If it hasn't, it's passive. The latter remains in listening pending the allocation of new CCN nodes. Our architecture is made up of these main actors: SDN orchestrator, SDN controller, CCN node, CCN server, and CCN client. Figure 3 describes our architecture.

CCN client: It is an end-device to request data store and/or retrieval. The consumer connects via a DASH client that implements a native CCN interface. It is assumed that CCN client has a Personal storage to cache data.

CCN Server: It is a DASH server that provides different video segments with various representations.

CCN node: (described in Subsect. 4.4). It can be a Border Node (BR) responsible for communications between different areas, an Edge node (EN) is a node to which a client device is connected to and In-network node (IN) is a node which located within the network. It is assumed that EN and IN basically has a storage to cache data. BR is responsible for the interconnection between the autonomous systems.

SDN Controller: (described in Subsect. 4.5). It has a local network vision of its supervised area. It communicates CCN nodes through extended OpenFlow messages to be informed of network conditions. It installs rules in CCN nodes to reach the requested content through an optimized path. Area Controller participates to caching/replacement processing.

SDN Orchestrator: (described in Subsect. 4.5). To ensure scalability, we introduce SDN orchestrator. It has a global network vision of all area controllers that are associated. It allows communication and exchanges between area controllers.

4.2 RF-VS-SD-CCN Operating Principle

Our architecture allows active cooperation between the different elements of the network. CCN nodes, SDN controllers and SDN Orchestrator pushing the DASH client to make a good selection of segments in order to have the convenient quality of network conditions as well as client capacities.

Table 2. CCN and SDN vs SD-CCN

ICN /CCN : Strenghts and Drawbacks
(+) Control and data forwarding functions are decoupled.
(+) Forwarding decisions are content based.
(+) Network automatically interprets processes and delivers content independently of its locations.
(+) Network replica routing.
(+) In-network caching.
(+) Self-certifying names.
(-) Clean slate concepts/architecture
(-) Flooding strategy for forwarding
(-) Network traffic increases

SDN : Strenghts and Drawbacks
(+) Control and data planes are decoupled.
(+) Forwarding decision are flow based.
(+) Providing a programmable network platform to implement and deploy new applications and architectures.
(+) Improving performance with a global network view and a feedback control with information exchanged between different layers in the network architecture.
(+) An external entity, the controller responsible for the control function of resources and abstractions.
(-) Flexibility: creating a new path generates an additional control overhead
(-) Reliability: the convergence time increases with the size of the network

			SD-CCN : Motivations and Challenges				
	Naming	Routing	Caching	Security	Fault tolerance	Network programmable	Network global view
CCN	Named Data Object	Content based	Native support	Self-certifying names	ICN nodes distributed	Not supported	Needs cooperation
SDN	Domain Name System	Flow based	Not supported	Secured communication channels	Logically centralized so critical	Native support	Native support

In [27, 28], the authors detailed when users shared similar video preferences the probability of requesting the same video content is higher too. First, we introduce the new concept of "family" defined by analyzing the user preference similarity (e.g. playback time, delay margin) and mobility similarity (e.g. movement direction and moving speed), which can help improve routing performance and cache hit ratio in mobile networks. Subsequently, we propose a CCN process which consists of Traffic Shaping and Interests anticipation, as well as SDN controller process that enables path optimization, caching, and replication decisions. These features help maintain the stability of high-quality DASH traffic.

4.3 Metrics Collection

To the best of our knowledge, the study of improving QoE of a SD-CCN architecture is not well studied. In the literature, we find a single approach in [22] where the authors proposed a hybrid SDN-CCN architecture with DASH to improve QoE based on bandwidth measurements for adaptation rate in order to improve QoS on the network side and QoE on the client side. This solution did not take into account the user mobility which characterizes most of today's Internet users as well as their preferences to satisfy them and consequently improve QoE. For this, we then propose to collect the necessary information which can influence the QoS on the network side and the QoE on the client side.

Metrics Collection in the Client Side
To build a user family, two key factors are taken into consideration; estimation of the user preferences similarity pattern as well as estimation of the mobility similarity pattern of a mobile user. Firstly, the mobility similarity model of a mobile user is defined as follows:
Direction of mobility (MD): for each mobile user x, we present his movement information by a two-dimensional vector $s_x \Leftrightarrow (x_1, x_2)$. So, for any node x and node y the mobility similarity between them is calculated as in Eq. (1).

$$MD(s_x, s_y) = \frac{(x_1 y_1, x_2 y_2)}{\sqrt{x_1^2 + x_2^2} \cdot \sqrt{y_1^2 + y_2^2}} \tag{1}$$

Mobility Speed (MS): is used for requester to choose a transmit node x based on the family when routing the interest packet. It is defined by Eq. (2).

$$MS_x = \sqrt{x_1^2 + x_2^2} \tag{2}$$

Similar movement behavior is expected to enhance the success rate of looking up. Thus, we select users whose value of $MD(s_x, s_y) > \alpha$ as a candidate set, while the moving speed $MS_x > \delta$, where and is considered as an adjustable threshold.

Secondly, estimation of the **user preference similarity** pattern in CCMNs is also a major issue. Video playback history is considered in the assessment of user preference. However, in order to exploit the preference similarity of users, it is not enough to know the historical playback trajectory in mobile networks. By clustering similar items in historical playback library, we extract the playback time and popularity as user preference similarity. Different from traditional clustering pattern, two vital factors are considered by playback trace which plays a significant role in family construction.

Playback Time (PT): records the duration the user watched the videos. We first define a non-negative parameter $p_i^x (1 \leq i \leq k)$ as the preference user x has related to the video of type i. The formula is shown in Eq. (3) [28].

$$P_i^x = \sum_{ck_j \in CK_x} I_i(ck_j) \frac{P_x(ckj)}{P_{total}(ck_j)} \tag{3}$$

where CK_x defines the set of video chunks viewed by user x, $p_{total}(ck_j)$ and $p_x(ck_j)$ represent the length of the complete video and the duration of the video playback history respectively. $I_i(ck_j)$ indicates whether user x has watched type i video in a certain time. This indicator is defined in Eq. (4).

$$I_i(ck_j) = \begin{cases} 1 & if \ ck_j \in T_i \\ 0 & otherwise \end{cases} \tag{4}$$

$T_i\{t_1, t_2, \ldots, t_k\}$ represents the classification set for the video. Obviously, a higher p_i^x indicates that user x takes more time on the type video i, and is more likely to be interested in category i.

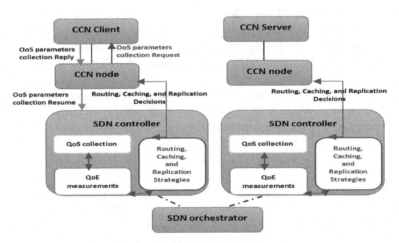

Fig. 3. RF-VS-SD-CCN architecture

Request Frequency (RF): Based on the requests popularity for all mobile users, we define the Request Frequency as a set of video popularity metrics that is calculated by a Zipf distribution [14]. We describe RF via $q(mi)$, where m_i is the popular rank of category i in CCMNs. To define the user preferences similarity of mobile users for each video type i, we based on the Term Frequency-Inverse Document Frequency (TF-IDF) principle. We set the preference W_i^x of a mobile user x for the video type i as follows:

$$W_i^x = TF_i^x IDF_i^x = \frac{P_i^x}{CK^x} \log \frac{1}{q(m_i)} \tag{5}$$

$$CK^x = \sum_{i=1}^{k} P_i^x \tag{6}$$

where p_i^x denotes the playback time of video type i and CK^x denotes the length of total video by mobile user x. $q(mi)$ denotes the request frequency of video type i in all users, which is obtained via RF.

Equation (7) presents a similarity weight normalization of preferences of each video type i for mobile user x:

$$w_i^x = \frac{W_i^x}{\sum_{i=1}^{k} W_i^x} \tag{7}$$

We define β as an adjustable threshold and assume that each mobile node has its own reference. Based on the threshold β, we select the nodes whose values of $w_i^x > \beta$ as the candidate associate nodes.

Finally, each family F is presented by the following data structure as follows:

$$<VN, T_i, MD, MS, PT, RF>$$

where VN is the name of the requested video. T_i defines video type. MD, MS, PT and RF denote the direction of the mobility, the mobility speed, th playback time and the request frequency, respectively.

Metrics Collection in the Network Side

Our proposal (RF-VS-SD-CCMN) is based on the QoS parameter collection module, the management module (routing, caching and replication decisions), and the QoE measurement module. The primary function of the first module is to provide real-time link QoS information for the QoE measurement module. The second module is responsible for controlling and calculating the QoE value of the transmission path in order to decide the final path to be selected. The management module uses the information collected and calculated by the other modules to make final routing, caching, and replication decisions. The operating mechanism is illustrated in Fig. 3.

In this article, we consider the following quality of service parameters: bandwidth, link occupancy, delay, packet loss rate, and jitter.

We define the path, as a finite sequence of nodes, between two distinct nodes i and j as follows: $\tau = \{n_o, n_1, \ldots, n_k\}$ such that $(n_i, n_1) \in L (0 \le i \le h - 1)$ where L represents set of the links. Let $\tau(i,j)$ presents each valid path between i and j and its length is $|\tau|$.

In order to estimate the bandwidth of a valid path, we need to calculate the bandwidth for each link included in the path. Note that the bandwidth between two linked ports of nodes i and j is determined by the minimum value of the bandwidth. So, we set the available bandwidth $B_p(\tau)$ as the maximum port bandwidth minus the port traffic. It is defined by Eq. (8).

$$B_p(\tau) = Min_{(0 \le i \le |\tau|-1)} B(\tau[i], \tau[i+1]) \tag{8}$$

To reach a destination on a path consists of several links, the delay is cumulative. The transit of an intermediate node adds a delay that can be defined as the delay time. This can be expressed as follows:

$$D_p(\tau) = \sum_{(0 \leq i \leq |\tau|-1)} D(\tau[i], \tau[i+1]) \qquad (9)$$

Jitter is a decisive parameter for evaluating the states of latency changes on a valid path. It can be calculated by subtracting current path delay from the previous path delay. We denote $J_p(\tau)$ *as jitter* described in Eq. (10) where k indicates the kth moment.

$$J_p(\tau) = E(|D_{k+1} - D_k|) \qquad (10)$$

Continuously monitoring the link rate per slot L_i and comparing it to the link capacity L_c allows the *Link Occupation Ratio* to be measured. $L_{OR}(\tau)$ can be calculated by the ratio of the difference between L_i and L_c to L_c. It is described in Eq. (11). However, the $L_{OR}(\tau)$ is high, the system will reduce the resolution of the video segments for future requests. This makes it possible to better adapt to changes in the network.

$$L_{OR}(\tau) = \sum_{(0 \leq i \leq |\tau|-1)} \frac{E(|L_i - L_c|)}{L_c} \qquad (11)$$

Packet Loss Rate: this metric can be defined by the total number of lost packets divided by the total number of the transmitted packet. Let $L_p(\tau)$ the packet loss rate, and it is defined by Eq. (12).

$$L_p(\tau) = 1 - \prod_{(0 \leq i \leq |\tau|-1)} 1 - L(\tau[i], \tau[i+1]) \qquad (12)$$

4.4 CCN Process

The main feature of CCN is in-network caching. However, this generates new problems such as flow oscillations [30]. To overcome the inefficiencies of caching, our proposal is based on supporting the mobile user to guide them towards the best choice through the different steps of the request and the transmission of the data packet. Therefore, the client rate adaptation choices are processed by the CCNs in order to accommodate the chunks already cached locally and their bitrates.

For this, the CCN node checks when receiving an interest packet whether the following video piece is cached locally and with which representation. If not, it checks first Family Storage Client Table (FSCT) which provides information about video chunks cached by clients of the same family. If the requested chunk is not yet found, then CCN node secondly checks Neighbor Storage Node Table (NSNT) which provides information on video chunks cached by other CCN nodes (Edge/Internal Node) requiring only on one hop for content delivery. Otherwise, it predicts future demand on the next video chunk to the assigned SDN controller, which improves QoE. The latter according to its complete vision on its coverage area, it determines the best route based on cooperative caching of assigned CCN nodes. Otherwise, it predicts a future demand on the next video segment to neighboring SDN controllers through its SDN orchestrator. Figure 5 described this principle.

The different functionalities of CCN are traffic shaping, anticipation of interests, cooperative caching and content replication according to utility (cost delivery).

Traffic Shaping

This step involves modifying the data rate provided based on mobile user observations. The flow rate noted T_{res} must verify the following conditions:

$$T_{res} \geq r_{req}B_s \leq T_{res} \leq B_c \tag{13}$$

T_{res} must be greater than or equal to the rate of the requested chunk. It must also be between the bandwidth on the server side with the CCN node (B_s) and the available bandwidth on the connection of the client side with the CCN node (B_c).

Interests Anticipation

To support DASH over CCN, CCN nodes should request a future chunk with a specified rate to achieve better QoE. Two constraints are addressed: the occupation of the buffer presented by the cache capacity of the CCN node and the available bandwidth (B_c/B_s).

$$r_{anticip} = \arg \min_{r_i, 1 \leq i \leq n} |r_i - B_s|. \tag{14}$$

Cooperative Caching

Due to limited space, our caching approach will be briefly described in this article, focusing on the main tables used for caching management. The SDN and CCN processes present an evolution of our preview work [24] of the study of caching for CCN networks. FSCT and NSNT tables, described in Fig. 4, are managed by SDN controllers. After creating user families and as the network traffic information is collected, SDN controller updates FSCT which records the information about the cached content in the personal storage of clients belonging to the same family. Based on the topology information collected, SDN controller fills NSNT with information from video content cached in neighbors requiring a one hop for content delivery.

Content Replication

Each SDN orchestrator manages a geographic area that consists of several neighboring SDN controllers and acts as a broker for them. In the event of multiple exchanges between SDN controllers to locate an interest packet and if a join request threshold is reached then the SDN orchestrator triggers a network information collection request without waiting for periodic network information collections. Then, it analyzes the topology, QoS collection, and content distribution. Finally, it installs rules for replication points taking into account QoE measurements.

4.5 SDN Process

According to the basic CCN approach when a data packet is transmitted, the intermediate CCN nodes store a copy of the content. This principle generates content redundancy in the network, frequent updating of caches and poor use of resources. Our hybrid architecture provides cooperative caching by leveraging the cache capacity of CCN nodes and the SDN controller's network vision to update cache cooperation tables between clients of the same family or neighboring nodes. Each SDN controller listens continuously to associated CCN nodes by monitoring network information collected periodically. Our proposal is based on an OpenFlow extension. There are three types of messages exchanged between the controller and the CCN nodes. The first is *symmetric* messages. Once the secure channel is established, **Hello** (Request/Reply) messages are exchanged. Then, **Echo** (Request/Reply) messages are used during channel operation to ensure the connection is still alive and to measure current latency and throughput. The second type is *asynchronous* messages which are sent by CCN nodes to the controller without the node having been requested by the controller. The **Packet-In** message is used to pass a packet for their support (content name lookup/routing information). The **Port-status** message is used to communicate link changes. Finally, the CCN node uses the **Error** message to notify the controller of errors. The last type is *controller-switch* messages which is the most important category. These messages may or may not require a response from the CCN node. **Feature-caching_replication** (Request/Reply) messages are used to enable caching which is managed by the controller.

With this new functionality added to the controller, data collection is mandatory to manage the caches scattered over the network. For this, **Read-state_cache** (Request/Reply) messages are used. According to collected information, **Modify-state** (Routing/Caching) messages are used to apply changes. The OpenFlow protocol messages described in this subsection are resumed in Table 3. Note that Packet-In and Modify-state messages are only executed after an unmatched incoming packet or its absence in CCN caches.

We consider a network represented by a finite and undirected graph $G(N, A)$, where N represents the set of nodes while A defines the links between them $|N| = n$ and $|A| = a$. Let's P the optimal path between a sequence of nodes, while z defines the length of the path. $(n_i; n_{i+1} \in A, \forall i = (1, \dots, z-1)$. For each link, we define an associated bandwidth $B_z \geq 0$ and a delay $\Delta_z \geq 0$. Our goal is to reach the path P having the maximum link capacity and the minimum path length. P_{ac} defines the capacity of the links of the path P.

$$P_{AC} = Max \sum_{i=1}^{z-1} B_{ai}; P = Min \sum_{i=0}^{N} a_z \qquad (15)$$

5 Performance Evaluation

5.1 Simulation Setup and Parameters

We perform a set of extensive simulations in an extended mininet emulation environment to emulate very large SDN networks (e.g. Maxinet), a wide area network simulator supporting DASH to simulate the data transmission procedure in CCMN (e.g. ndnsim in NS3), and a traffic generator to generate a traffic flow.

Content Store (CS)	Pending Interest Table (PIT)	Forwarding Information Base (FIB)	FSCT /NSNT			
			Video Chunk ID	Video File ID	Encoding Bitrate	Node ID

Fig. 4. CCN node tables

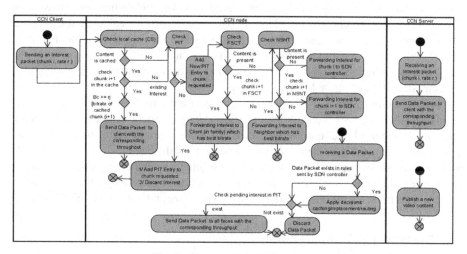

Fig. 5. Flowchart of CCN process

We have developed our own implementation of FESTIVE [33] in order to simulate the adaptation behavior on the client side. Its principle is to capture the latest advances in bitrate adaptation based on the occupation of the buffer memory. The videos consist of 2 s segments. User interests are captured by a Zipf type distribution (controlled via the asymmetry parameter α). We use YouTube recommended encoding rates. CCN server codes each video with 4 different bitrates (1, 2.5, 5 and 8). The control of any segment of the video is entrusted to FESTIVE as soon as a request is triggered.

To emulate large SDN networks, we use MaxiNet which extends the Mininet emulation environment to cover emulation on multiple physical machines. We realize an SDN network by 1 orchestrator and 3 controllers. Next, we instantiate 30 nodes (CCN). The number of mobile users for any CCN node (EN) is limited to 5. We choose 20 Mbps for the link capacity since this value is dedicated for adaptive streaming.

Three additional caching schemes are evaluated with RF-VS-SD-CCMN for comparison. Cache Everything Everywhere (default CCN) [17, 32], is a reference in the literature. ProbCache [32] is used to compare our work to a probabilistic caching model [29]. DASH-SDN-CCN [22] is chosen to evaluate a caching model for video streaming based on an SD-CCN architecture. Table 4 presents the simulation parameters.

Each CCN (EN/IN) node has a Content Store (CS). The size C_i is controlled by ω and it is related to a total available system capacity. We define C_i the capacity of each CCNnode with content store as:

$$C_i = \frac{\sum video\ size}{\#of\ CCN\ node}\omega i \in N, \tag{16}$$

The following parameters are used to evaluate the performance of RF-VS-SD-CCMN.

Expected Bitrate (E_b): It is an aggregation of successive measurements of the video quality that the user expects. It is presented in Fig. 8 (a1–b1)

Bitrate oscillation (B_o): in practice, it is presented by images indicating an improvement or a decrease in the quality of the video. In our experiments, we calculate the average of the number of increases and decreases in bitrate while viewing a video file. Figure 8 (a2–b2) draws an average of measurements of this parameter.

Video Freezing Duration (V_F): it can be defined as the average playback time spent in a "frozen" state. It is illustrated in Fig. 8 (a3–b3).

To evaluate our proposed work, we have chosen these measures to: *i)* control and evaluate on the client side the amount of average video that can be estimated by a mobile node (E_b). *ii)* control and monitor the bit rate oscillation on the client side in order to adapt to the client's requirements (B_o). *iii)* Finally, we calculate the duration of a video paused in the buffer memory in order to assess whether the choice of video bitrates by users is good (V_F). We run a set of repetitive evaluations by modifying the values of ω and α to determine the influence of total content store size and popularity-related bias α.

5.2 The Impact on Expected Bitrate

The ratio of bitrates selected by adaptive rate control during the entire experiment can be summarized by a bit rate distribution. This distribution reflects an aggregate measure of overall video quality that current network resources can support under a given caching replacement approach. We further use the weighted average to calculate the expected bitrate (E_b) based on the appearance of the bitrates in user requests, which maps the discrete rates to a continuous and comparable metric. A higher E_b indicates better cache efficiency by improving adaptive broadcast quality (Fig. 6).

Unlike the default CCN, all popularity-based strategies perform as well across different popularity distribution and cache-capacity. Figure 8(a1) shows that our proposal reached, at low cache capacity and high popularity asymmetry, E_b 14% higher than ProbCache and 33.1% better than default CCN. This proves the effectiveness of our caching strategy. In Fig. 8 (b1), when changes from 0.6 to 1.2 the expected video quality is improved for all caching strategies. We can deduce that user demands are focused on small set of popular content with larger α value. This increases the cache hit rate.

5.3 The Impact on Bitrate Oscillation

Figure 8(a2–b2) shows that bitrate switches increase with high cache capacity or decrease popularity distribution. Comparing our proposal with the other strategies, we notice that it achieves the lowest bitrate oscillations. This improves the cache hit rate and thus triggers bitrate adaptations to match the requested quality level. So, our caching system is based on an effective strategy that keeps user requests for high quality content as long as possible.

Table 3. Highlighted OpenFlow protocol messages

Message	Source	Destination	Role
Symmetric			
Hello-request			hand-shake Request (secure channel)
Hello-reply	Controller	Controller	hand-shake Reply (secure channel)
Echo-request	or	or	latency / throughput measurements Request
Echo-reply	CCN node	CCN node	latency / throughput measurements Reply
Asynchronous			
Packet-In			inform about the incoming packets (name lookup / routing information)
	CCN node	Controller	
Ports-status			indicate link changes
Error			notify the controller of errors
Controller-switch			
Feature-caching_replication-request			request to enable caching/replication functions
Read-state_cache-request	Controller	CCN node	collect the cached content in Content store
Read-state_routing-table-request			collect the routing table in FIB
Modify-state_cache-request			install rules for caching
Modify-state_routing-table-request			install rules for routing
Feature-caching_replication-reply			acceptance response for enabling caching / replication functions
Read-state_cache-reply	CCN node	Controller	send a summary for cached content in Content store
Read-state_routing-table-reply			send a summary for routes in FIB

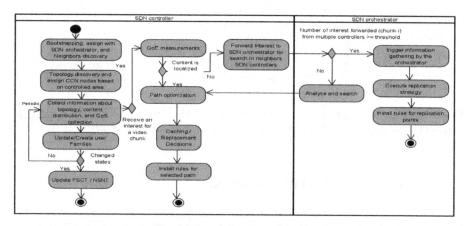

Fig. 6. Flowchart of SDN process

5.4 The Impact on Video Freezing

As long as the video access time for each video chunk is high, as long as the probability of freezing video playback is high. With a caching scheme that achieves a high success rate, the access time to the video chunk is reduced and subsequently the playback freeze is reduced. Figure 8 (c1–c2) shows the efficiency of our proposal. It achieves the least video freezing. This can be explained by the high success rate, maintaining user demands for high quality content and responding to requests as soon as possible to relieve the traffic load.

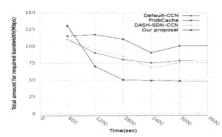

Fig. 7. Total amount for required bandwidth

Table 4. Simulation parameters

Parameter	Value
Number of video files	20
Number of video chunks per file	15
Number of CCN nodes	30
Video chunk playback time	2 sec
Encoded bitrates	{1, 2.5, 5, 8}
Bandwidth	20 Mbps
Skewness factor (α)	0.8
Content store size percentage (ω)	0.1

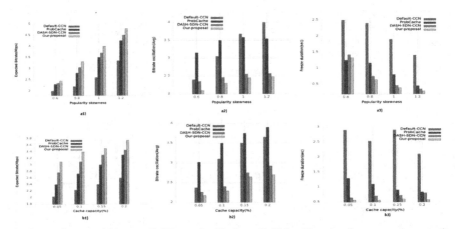

Fig. 8. a1) Expected bitrate a2) Bitrate Oscillation a3) Video Freezing [across cache capacity (ω)] b1) Expected bitrate b2) Bitrate Oscillation b3) Video Freezing [across popularity skewness (α)]

5.5 The Impact on Required Peak Bandwidth

To ensure seamless streaming delivery our proposal reduces underflow and buffer time. For this, as shown in Fig. 7, our proposal achieves the lowest peak bandwidth required.

6 Conclusion

The purpose of this article is to study the integration of SDN and CCN architectures for video streaming applications. Our application domain is mobile networks which also increase the characteristics to be taken into consideration mainly the mobility of users. Our proposal consists in creating families of users according to the similarity of mobility as well as the similarity of their preferences. As and when users send requests for video content, two additional processes will be executed; CCN process and SDN process. In order to obtain a close retrieval of content and fast video routing, we optimize the caching/replication mechanisms according to the controller's network vision. We have carried out numerous simulations to evaluate the performance of the proposed framework. The results show the effectiveness of the proposed framework based on the cooperation between CCN nodes with supervision controlled by the SDN controller for rapid routing of video chunks in the event of absence of requested content in local cache.

References

1. Koponen, T., et al.: A data-oriented (and beyond) network architecture. SIGCOMM Comput. Commun. Rev. **37**(4), 181–192 (2007)
2. Liu, Z., Dong, M., Gu, B.: Impact of item popularity and chunk popularity in CCN caching management. In: 18th Asia-Pacific Network Operations and Management Symposium (APNOMS), pp. 1–6. IEEE (2016)
3. Heiko, S., Detlev, M., Thomas, W.: Overview of the scalable video coding extension of the H. 264/AVC standard. IEEE Trans. Circuits Syst. Video Technol. **17**(9), 1103–1120 (2007)
4. Hu, F., Hao, Q., Bao, K.: A survey on software-defined network and OpenFlow: from concept to implementation. IEEE Commun. Surv. Tutor. **16**(4), 2181–2206 (2014)
5. Chanda, A., Westphal, C.: ContentFlow: adding content primitives to software defined networks. In: 2013 IEEE Global Communications Conference (GLOBECOM), pp. 2132–2138. IEEE, December 2013
6. Chang, D., Kwak, M., Choi, N., Kwon, T., Choi, Y.: C-flow: an efficient content delivery framework with OpenFlow. In: The International Conference on Information Networking 2014 (ICOIN2014), pp. 270–275. IEEE, February 2014
7. Luo, H., Cui, J., Chen, Z., Jin, M., Zhang, H.: Efficient integration of software defined networking and information-centric networking with CoLoR. In: 2014 IEEE Global Communications Conference, pp. 1962–1967. IEEE, December 2014
8. Gao, S., Zeng, Y., Luo, H., Zhang, H.: Scalable area-based hierarchical control plane for software defined information centric networking. In: 2014 23rd International Conference on Computer Communication and Networks (ICCCN), pp. 1–7. IEEE, August 2014
9. Shailendra, S., Panigrahi, B., Rath, H.K., Simha, A.: A novel overlay architecture for information centric networking. In: 2015 Twenty First National Conference on Communications (NCC), pp. 1–6. IEEE, February 2015
10. Famaey, J., et al.: On the merits of svc-based http adaptive streaming. In: 2013 IFIP/IEEE International Symposium on Integrated Network Management (IM 2013), pp. 419–426, May 2013
11. Sanchez, Y., et al.: iDASH: improved dynamic adaptive streaming over http using scalable video coding. In: Proceedings of the Second Annual ACM Conference on Multimedia Systems, New York, NY, USA, 2011, MMSys 2011, pp. 257–264. ACM (2011)
12. Sanchez, Y., et al.: Efficient HTTP-based streaming using scalable video coding. Signal Process. Image Commun. **27**(4), 329–342 (2012)
13. Lederer, S., Mueller, C., Timmerer, C., Hellwagner, H.: Adaptive multimedia streaming in information-centric networks. IEEE Netw. **28**(6), 91–96 (2014)
14. Yu, Y., Bronzino, F., Fan, R., Westphal, C., Gerla, M.: Congestion-aware edge caching for adaptive video streaming in information-centric networks. In: IEEE Consumer Communications & Networking Conference (CCNC) (2015)
15. Liu, C., Bouazizi, I., Gabbouj, M.: Parallel adaptive HTTP media streaming. In: 2011 Proceedings of 20th International Conference on Computer Communications and Networks (ICCCN), pp. 1–6. IEEE, July 2011
16. Andelin, T., Chetty, V., Harbaugh, D., Warnick, S., Zappala, D.: Quality selection for dynamic adaptive streaming over http with scalable video coding. In: Proceedings of the 3rd Multimedia Systems Conference, New York, NY, USA, 2012, MMSys 2012, pp. 149–154. ACM (2012)

17. Jacobson, V., Smetters, D.K., Hornton, J.D., Plass, M.F., Briggs, N.H., Braynard, R.L.: Networking named content. In: Proceedings of ACM CoNEXT (2009)
18. Kleinrouweler, J.W., Cabrero, S., Cesar, P.: Delivering stable high-quality video: an SDN architecture with DASH assisting network elements. In: MMSys 2016, Klagenfurt, Austria (2016)
19. Cofano, G., De Cicco, L., Zinner, T., Nguyen-Ngoc, A., Tran-Gia, P., Mascolo, S.: Design and experimental evaluation of network-assisted strategies for HTTP adaptive streaming. In: MMSys 2016, Klagenfurt, Austria (2016)
20. Naman, A.T., Wang, Y., Gharakheili, H.H., Sivaraman, V., Taubman, D.: Responsive high throughput congestion control for interactive applications over SDN-enabled networks. Comput. Netw. **134**, 152–166 (2018)
21. Georgopoulos, P., Broadbent, M., Farshad, A., Plattner, B., Race, N.: Using software defined networking to enhance the delivery of video-on-demand. Comput. Commun. **69**, 79–87 (2015)
22. Jmal, R., Chaari Fourati, L.: Assisted DASH-aware networking over SDN–CCN architecture. Photonic Netw. Commun. **38**(1), 37–50 (2019). https://doi.org/10.1007/s11107-019-00835-1
23. Fekih, A., Fantar, S.G., Youssef, H.: SDN-based replication management framework for CCN networks. In: Workshops of the International Conference on Advanced Information Networking and Applications, pp. 83–99. Springer, Cham, April 2020
24. Fekih, A., Fantar, S.G., Youssef, H.: Secure SDN-based in-network caching scheme for CCN. In: 13th International Conference on Systems and Networks Communications (ICSNC), pp. 21–28, October 2018
25. Fekih, A., Gaied, S., Youssef, H.: Proactive content caching strategy with router reassignment in content centric networks based SDN. In: 2018 IEEE 11th Conference on Service-Oriented Computing and Applications (SOCA), pp. 81–87. IEEE, November 2018
26. Li, W., Sharief, O., Fayed, M., Hassanein, H.S.: Bitrate adaptation-aware cache partitioning for video streaming over information-centric networks. In: 2018 IEEE 43rd Conference on Local Computer Networks (LCN), pp. 401–408. IEEE, October 2018
27. Xu, C., Jia, S., Zhong, L., Muntean, G.M.: Socially aware mobile peer-to-peer communications for community multimedia streaming services. IEEE Commun. Mag. **53**(10), 150–156 (2015)
28. Wang, M., Xu, C., Jia, S., Guan, J., Grieco, L.A.: Preference-aware fast interest forwarding for video streaming in information-centric VANETs. In: 2017 IEEE International Conference on Communications (ICC), pp. 1–7. IEEE, May 2017
29. He, Q., Chang, K., Lim, E.P., Banerjee, A.: Keep it simple with time: a reexamination of probabilistic topic detection models. IEEE Trans. Pattern Anal. Mach. Intell. **32**(10), 1795–1808 (2010)
30. Lee, D.H., Dovrolis, C., Begen, A.C.: Caching in HTTP adaptive streaming: friend or foe? In: Proceedings of Network and Operating System Support on Digital Audio and Video Workshop, pp. 31–36, March, 2014
31. Wang, Y., Orapinpatipat, C., Gharakheili, H.H., Sivaraman, V.: TeleScope: flow-level video telemetry using SDN. In: 2016 Fifth European Workshop on Software-Defined Networks (EWSDN), Den Haag, Netherlands, pp. 31–36 (2016)
32. Alkhazaleh, M., Aljunid, S., Sabri, N.: A review of caching strategies and its categorizations in information centric network. J. Theor. Appl. Inf. Technol. **97**(19) (2019)
33. Jiang, J., Sekar, V., Zhang, H.: Improving fairness, efficiency, and stability in HTTP-based adaptive video streaming with festive. In: Proceedings of the 8th International Conference on Emerging Networking Experiments and Technologies, pp. 97–108, December 2012

Leveraging SDN for Smart City Applications Support

Emna Rbii[✉] and Imen Jemili[ID]

Faculty of Sciences of Bizerte, University of Carthage, Carthage, Tunisia
rbiiemna@gmail.com, imen.jmili@fsb.u-carthage.tn

Abstract. Recently, Software Defined Network (SDN) paradigm has been viewed as a promising solution that can help creating and designing more efficient intelligent solutions for smart city projects. By splitting the control and data planes, SDN presents an efficient methodology to overcome compatibility, interoperability and scalability issues. In this paper, we introduce the smart city concept and further conduct an analysis of the challenges facing smart cities. We also present a general overview of research that focuses on leveraging the benefits of software-defined networking in specific applications domains of smart cities that has been carried out to date. Furthermore, we discuss the associated potential issues that need to be addressed.

Keywords: Software defined network · Smart cities · Smart grid · VANETs

1 Introduction

According to the United Nations [1], the number of people living in cities by 2050 is estimated to 6 billion due to population growth and migration [2]. And with the increase in urbanization and its associated problems such as waste management, air pollution, human health concerns and traffic congestions, the interest in smart city concept is growing worldwide and many cities, with diverse needs, are moving towards the realization of the smart cities concept, like Songdo in South Korea, Masdar city in Abu Dhabi and Lavasa in India [3]. Recent advances in networking, telecommunications, information and communication technologies (ICTs), along with the advent of IoT [4], have contributed to the emergence and realization of this concept [2,5]. Indeed, the digitalization of urban systems and the ubiquity of the Internet have brought fundamental changes in the way citizens live and the way cities are governed in recent years. Smart cities provide many opportunities ahead through building a sustainable urban environment and improving the quality of life for citizens. With sensing and automation capabilities of deployed smart devices, a huge amount of data is collected from the physical environments, processed and analyzed to offer citizens personalized services and applications, get their feedback and imply them more, as they are the main catalyst that accelerates smart city initiatives. Billions of smart

© Springer Nature Switzerland AG 2020
I. Jemili and M. Mosbah (Eds.): DiCES-N 2020, CCIS 1348, pp. 95–119, 2020.
https://doi.org/10.1007/978-3-030-65810-6_6

devices and sophisticated sensor and ICT technologies are required to offer a global networked communication infrastructure, which must be coupled with data analytics and interpretation system to handle gathered data and provide valuable services and continuous monitoring and tracking of the environment. However, several challenges hinder the realization of the Smart City Concept on a large scale, mainly related to the heterogeneity of devices and applications, scalability, security and privacy [2,6–8]. To effectively address these problems, several emerging technologies such as cloud computing, fog computing, Network Function Virtualization (NFV), Software-Defined Networks (SDNs) can bring a new perspective to the development of smart city projects [9], for example by enabling a more effective management of connected devices or a better handling and analysis of collected data. In this context, we will focus on the deployment of SDN in the context of smart city applications and how it has been leveraged to address some of the challenges inherent in smart cities. The main idea of SDN paradigm is to design flexible and programmable network architecture [10]. Indeed, it decouples the data plane from the control plane in order to facilitate the deployment of new protocols and applications and simplify network management, by keeping the intelligence of the network at the controller level while the network devices (switches and routers) become simple transmission devices. Although many surveys and researches have explored the SDN concept, each of them has addressed a specific problem in this area. In [10] and [11], the focus is on the presentation of SDN paradigm. The authors detail the intrinsic characteristics of SDN, its architecture and its main components compared to traditional networks. In [12], the authors identify the main fault management issues in SDN and provide a classification according to the affected layers, mainly infrastructure, control and application layers. They also reviewed state of the art approaches that address those issues. As the network visibility at the logically centralized controller is a unique characteristic of SDN, in [13], the authors tackled the topology discovery and its associated security implications by discussing possible threats relevant to each layer. In order to select the most appropriate QoS routing algorithm for a particular use case, authors in [14] have studied the centralized QoS routing mechanisms in SDN and introduced a novel four-dimensional (4D) evaluation framework. Some surveys focused on the deployment of SDN in a specific context. [15] and [16] investigate how SDN is used in VANETs by presenting its generic architecture and identifying their advantages and impacts. In addition, they focused on the challenges of SDN enabled Vehicular Network (SDVN) in terms of reliability and security. In [17], Rehmani et al. present how SDN has been integrated into smart power grids by detailing its architectures and benefits, and discuss its contributions in terms of routing and security. In [18], the authors present the various works that have implemented SDN to facilitate network management in smart homes. None of the aforementioned surveys provide a general overview of how the SDN has been exploited in the context of smart city applications. The main contributions of this survey are:

– Providing an overview of smart city concept by outlining its applications and challenges.
– Presenting how SDN has been exploited in smart city applications and highlighting its contributions.

This paper is organized as follows. Section 2 will present the methodology used to conduct this review. Section 3 briefly introduces the Smart City concept and details its applications and challenges. Section 4 presents the SDN concept and provides an overview of Smart City applications that have exploited the SDN, followed by a discussion. Finally, Sect. 5 gives a conclusion and open perspectives.

2 Methodology

In this section, we will explain the methodology adopted to conduct this review. As illustrated in Fig. 1, three main steps are required:

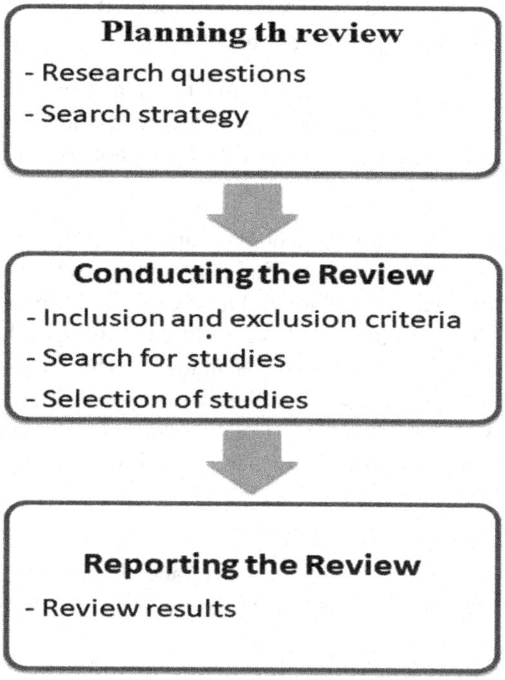

Fig. 1. Methodology steps

Planning the Review
The objective of this paper is to study how SDN has been exploited in smart city applications. In this regard, we have followed a research approach based on the following questions:

- How has SDN been deployed in smart city applications?
- What are the benefits of leveraging the SDN for smart city applications?
- What are the open issues to be addressed for SDN-based solutions?

To search and collect the most relevant studies to our topic, we used the most popular scientific databases, namely: Institute of Electrical and Electronics Engineers (IEEE), Springer, Elsevier Scopus, Wiley, and Association for Computing Machinery ACM Digital Library.

Conducting the Review
We have focused our research on smart city applications that have exploited the SDN. We used the following search terms: "SDN-based solutions", "smart city application", "smart grids", "VANETs", "e-health", "smart economy", "smart industry", "challenges", and "smart cities". These keywords were combined to tune the search. Once the primary articles are identified and collected, an in-depth analysis of each article is done to evaluate and select the most relevant ones, from 2014 up to 2020. To do so, selection criteria (inclusion and exclusion criteria) must be set based on the research questions. At least one of the following inclusion criteria must be met to retain an article:

- Proposing an SDN based solution for smart city applications.
- Tackling the use of SDN in a specific smart city application.
- Surveys dealing with SDN as an innovative technology for smart city applications.

Any other document that does not meet the above inclusion criteria and has one of the following criteria: not written in English, exploits SDN in a field other than smart city applications will be excluded. Thus, we will obtain a new collection of documents. At this level, duplicates from different bibliographic databases will be identified and removed. A selection is made on the basis of title, abstract and keywords. Afterwards, a selection based on the reading of the full-text is made for each study. References that do not meet the inclusion criteria will be excluded. Following these steps, we obtain the primary articles from which we will extract the data for our paper.

Reporting the Review
This step consists of exploiting the data extracted from the selected primary documents to answer the various questions mentioned above and write the article.

3   Smart Cities: An Overview

Recently, the Smart City concept has been proposed as a powerful tool to overcome challenges facing cities and transform them into more prosperous and liveable places [3,5]. Despite its popularity and the growing interest in this concept, there is still no common general definition of this paradigm and it is referred to by alternative terms such as "smart city", "digital city", "knowledge city" [19].

In [20], the authors defined this concept while focusing on its objectives: "*Smart Cities initiatives try to improve urban performance by using data, information and information technologies (IT) to provide more efficient services to citizens, to monitor and optimize existing infrastructure, to increase collaboration among different economic actors, and to encourage innovative business models in both the private and public sectors.*" This definition, in accordance with other proposed ones [21], underlines the key role of information and communication technologies (ICT) in the implementation of smart city projects. In fact, to improve a city's economic, social and environmental sustainability, actions are required at many levels [22]. Smart cities will serve:

Citizens: The smart city takes an interest in its citizens by giving priority to their development and offering them several smart services to make their quality of life more comfortable.

Government: Smart city seeks to strengthen the relationships and interactions between government and urban stakeholders. In order to increase transparency and trust, it is important to improve the quality of services provided, enable access to government information and involve all stakeholders in decision-making.

Economy: Smart City aims to strengthen economic development. Indeed, it is useful to offer favourable conditions and follow new strategies to attract new businesses and increase employability.

Environment: Rapid industrialization and urbanization have caused enormous environmental problems, particularly in terms of pollution. In this context, smart city focuses on providing environmental solutions to reduce pollution and manage natural resources in a sustainable way.

To achieve these goals, many applications have been developed in many domains. In the following subsections, we will present the key smart city applications and the challenges encountered.

3.1   Smart City Applications

As the smart city focuses on meeting the needs of citizens and the city, a plethora of smart applications have emerged in various domains [23]. Many classifications have been proposed to categorise these applications, with focus on generic or specific aspects, such as technological aspect [24–26], humain aspect [27], institutional aspect [28]. In [29], Giffinger et al. have subdivided them into six main categories:

Smart Economy: Smart economy aims to improve the overall business climate by providing innovative ideas, which increase the productivity and reduce costs, providing opportunities and suitable conditions to support the creation and growth of businesses as well as new jobs [3,30]. It should encourage sustainable growth, while promoting a low-carbon, resource-efficient and competitive economy.

Smart People: Human capital plays a fundamental role in the process of building smart cities. Thus, cities must provide the conditions for long learning, social and ethnic plurality and flexibility, and promote creativity and participation in public life [3,30]. Programs and services for inhabitants must be provided to strengthen social capital and qualification, such as:

- E-education: It relies on the extensive use of modern ICT tools in public schools in order to enhance the students' wellbeing and encourage them to look after their studies and education [31].
- Human capital management: It refers to policies aiming at improving investment in human capital, attracting and retaining new talents to serve the city by creating an appropriate environment for them to flourish and excel.

Smart Governance: To achieve integrated, transparent, open and cooperative governance, the government follows clear strategies and perspectives to support sustainable urban development for all. Besides, it offers innovative services to all stakeholders, citizens, businesses and other civil society organizations, in order to strengthen their participation in public management and transparent decision-making processes [30,32]. Many solutions are proposed to achieve these objectives, mainly through online platforms and social media, such as:

- E-government: Thanks to ICTs, e-government services are available to all stakeholders to optimize work and ensure fast and quality services [33].
- E-democracy: It also exploits ICTs to strengthen public participation in political life, for example in elections and referendums [34].

Smart Mobility: Reducing pollution and traffic congestion [35,36], increasing personal safety [37] and reducing transfer costs are the main objectives of intelligent mobility. More and more applications and services are being developed to promote safe and smart mobility while reducing the number of accidents and associated fatalities and injuries, as well as the $CO2$ footprint. They also aim to enhance the experience of drivers and citizens [22,30].

Smart Environment: The pollution problems and the increase in energy consumption are mainly related to the continuous growth of population and the expansion of cities. Nowadays, a considerable effort is being made to take care of the environment and relieve such issues. The aim is to protect the environment and conserve natural resources by using them in a sustainable and economic way [30,38]. To offer and maintain a healthy environment, many applications are proposed, such as:

- Smart grid: The main objective of smart grid is to increase the electrical system's efficiency, dependability and flexibility. It adapts the production and distribution of electrical energy to demands in an automatic and autonomous way. Sensors networks and real-time data analysis systems are deployed to monitor and control the production and consumption of electricity and enable operators and users to make decisions when necessary [23,39].

- Smart lighting: This intelligent system uses the information collected by the sensors as weather conditions to autonomously adapt and control the lighting intensity according to the context, resulting in user-centric lighting, energy savings and reduced maintenance and operating costs [22,40].
- Green energy: It derives energy from regenerative natural resources in order to reduce environmental pollution [7].

Smart Living: Ensuring a more comfortable and sustainable living is one of the main objectives of smart cities. In this regard, smart living covers all aspects related to the citizens' live, ranging from health conditions, education facilities, individual safety, housing quality and social cohesion. It also targets cultural facilities to improve the quality of life for residents, to facilitate their interaction and integration into their environment, and to enhance the experience of visitors [3,30]. The main applications in this category are:

- E-health: It relies on networking and smart technologies to provide innovative solutions for health monitoring, information access and healthcare. The aim is to prevent, diagnose and treat the health status of people in real time [41–43] and to ensure a better quality of life for elderly people.
- Smart homes and smart buildings: They are built applying the most modern technologies in energy saving architecture, communications and access control in order to increase security and safety, save energy, time, and money and give more comfort to inhabitants [22,44,45]. Through connected sensors and control devices such as air conditioning, heating, ventilation and lighting, residents are able to track domestic information and regulate the settings of their smart home.

3.2   Challenges for Smart Cities

Although the smart city concept has become popular and widely accepted, its implementation in the real world still faces a number of challenges and issues. Several surveys have addressed the challenges of smart cities in a general way. In [2], the authors presented the challenges of smart cities and discussed the different opportunities and requirements to settle in the city of tomorrow. To implement a smart city effectively, the authors, in [7], presented the main challenges for its design. In [8], the authors explained the challenges that cities are facing to become smart cities. Other surveys focused on a specific challenge, such as security and privacy. In [46], Sookhak et al. tackled the different security and privacy requirements for a smart city, while identifying solutions. In [6], the authors discussed the security and privacy challenges related to some smart city applications, like intelligent healthcare, transportation, and smart energy. This sub-section presents the main challenges in the context of smart city applications:

Security and Privacy: As a complex ecosystem based on IoT, smart cities rely on detecting and gathering data from billions of heterogeneous smart devices deployed in various fields, such as smart transportation, e-health, smart agriculture, etc. [23,42,43,47]. Crowdsensing an other mean to collect diverse information. In fact, devices equipped with intelligent detection devices have become ubiquitous, such as smartphones, wearable devices and tablets. Being an excellent source of information when used by a large number of users, they offer higher coverage and better context awareness [6,48]. This huge collected volume of data, including highly sensitive citizen information, such as user's identity, location or health condition, are vulnerable to many security threats [49,50]. Data is gathered through diverse shared infrastructures relying on heterogeneous communication systems vulnerable to various attacks; many weaknesses stemmed from wireless sensor networks, main platform to sense and collect data [51]. For all these reasons, updated security countermeasures must be deployed to protect privacy and build secure and stable smart cities [6,49].

Heterogeneity: Smart cities infrastructure that collects data is constituted of a wide variety of smart devices, network access technologies, communication protocols and platforms, which are multi-functional and multi-vendor [7,52]. As this heterogeneity hinders interoperability at the application layer, the ability to integrate these heterogeneous components is considered as a critical issue for the concept of smart cities and needs to be addressed as a priority [49,53]. To overcome this obstacle, it is essential to design standards that ensure transparent integration of devices and software as well as minimize incompatibilities with legacy devices and systems [7,54].

Scalability: Smart cities are rapidly developing from small testbeds to large-scale implementations, resulting in explosive growth in both data and network traffic. Besides, with the rapid increase in number of smart devices coupled with the heterogeneity of devices, applications and interactions, scalability is becoming a primary challenge for the large-scale deployment of sensors and sensing environments, for the processing of structured and unstructured data gathered from IoT devices and for their storage. Therefore, a smart city cannot work properly without scalable systems and mechanisms [50].

Connectivity: One of the key elements in a smart city project is to ensure a reliable, ubiquitous and seamless connectivity [55]. To enable data collection from diverse mobile devices, relying on wireless networks seems an efficient and cost-effective solution to offer connectivity to massively deployed devices, even in harsh or hostile environments where communication networks are missing. Since smart cities are based on a large number of heterogeneous smart devices, scattered over large areas, interacting with each other and exchanging data, the adoption of communication technology depends on several criteria, namely throughput (low or high speed), coverage (long or short range links), scalability, security, etc. [56,57]. Besides, connectivity issues may arise because existing technologies are designed only for a limited number of devices and for a specific communication range [53,57]. For this reason, it is worth designing a holistic and coherent architecture supporting connectivity from embedded CPSs (Cyber Physical Systems) to cloud where data storage and analysis are performed, while relying on diverse and heterogeneous communication platforms.

Big Data: Nowadays, data is considered as one of the most valuable assets for smart cities, capable of bringing both opportunities and new challenges to data analysis. In fact, smart cities are experiencing an exponential increase in the data generated by billions of connected devices of different kinds, including social networking platforms, environmental sensors, traffic counters, etc.; this data in different formats may be structured, unstructured and semi-structured. This massive data need to be analyzed to deduce relevant and useful information and to predict the future observations and to be stored for future exploitation. In order to make decisions and achieve sustainable development objectives, the different steps require scalable computing infrastructures for an effective and efficient data exploitation, while handling data complexity and data dependence. It is therefore essential to find effective solutions and mechanisms for the transfer, storage and analysis of this huge mass of data [2].

Cost: The realistic implementation of an intelligent city is very expensive due to the high cost of installation, operation and maintenance of the required infrastructures, in addition to the fees of IT professionals and consultants [58]. Therefore, cost is considered a very important factor in the deployment of the smart city and the sustainability of its daily operations later [7,50]. For this reason, cost optimization is a major challenge during the entire life cycle of a smart city [9].

To handle the increased complexity and requirements of smart cities, new emerging technologies have been deployed as key solutions to facilitate the implementation of smart city applications. These new paradigms, such as Cloud/fog computing, big data, software defined networks (SDN), network function virtualization (NFV), cognitive management, machine learning and blockchain, can bring a new perspective to smart city project developments [9,59]. For example, to support the massive amount of data generated by smart sensors, Big Data tools are used. Thanks to its data storage and processing capabilities, cloud computing presents itself as an enabling technology for complex smart city systems [59]. In this paper, we mainly focus on SDN. In the following section, we detail how SDN has been exploited to meet some of the requirements of smart city applications.

4 SDN for Smart Cities

With the advent of the Internet and new information technologies such as Big Data [60], Cloud Computing [61] and IoT [62], traditional networks are increasingly showing their weakness and posing great challenges to many operators and network administrators. In fact, the heterogeneity of deployed devices in current networks increases the complexity of the network management task, since each device operates according to specific protocols and has its own proprietary configuration; such a configuration must be translated through specific tools from high-level policies into low-level configuration commands while taking into account the dynamic state of the network [63]. Moreover, due to the lack of high-level language and appropriate tools, network operators are stuck with the rigidity of the current network infrastructure. Indeed, many control and management functions are implemented in the hardware and for this reason network devices are generally considered as closed black boxes. This strong coupling between the data plane and the control plane complicates network management, reduces flexibility and hinders innovation and evolution of the network infrastructure [10,11,64,65]. To overcome these limitations, the idea of programmable networks has been proposed in order to simplify network configuration and management[11]. In this context, Software Defined Networks have been introduced. This emerging paradigm decouples the control plane from data plane, allowing to alleviate the tasks of network devices and to shift the control of the overall network behaviour to the controller [64]. Thus, networking tasks become simpler and easier for network operators, who can deploy easily new protocols and applications in a centralized manner regardless of the different network hardware devices.

In the following subsections, we will introduce the SDN architecture and explain the benefits of SDN for smart city applications.

4.1 SDN Architecture

As depicted in Fig. 2, SDN architecture is divided into three major planes [66]:

Application Layer: The application layer includes end-user applications, such as security, routing, monitoring, etc. It provides an abstract view of the network and policies used to implement network control and operation logic. Through northbound Application Programming Interfaces (APIs), these policies are translated into instructions by the controller; via southbound APIs, the controller is able to program them directly on network equipment[10,65,66].

Control Layer: It is based on a logical entity, called controller. The controller is responsible for monitoring and managing network resources. The controller receives instructions from the application layer, transforms them into data processing rules and injects them into networking devices. It also extracts network information from data plane through the southbound API and supplies SDN applications with an abstract view of the network [10,65,66]. Different control models are proposed for the control plane [11,67]:

- Centralized model: It is a single entity, which has a global view of the network. It is responsible for managing all forwarding devices of the network. In large-scale and heterogeneous networks, such a single point of failure presents several issues, such as scalability, availability, reliability and performance.
- Distributed model: It allows sharing the control area between several controllers. Indeed, the control plane is partitioned into several controllers, physically distributed over the network, and each one has an over- knowledge of its region. Such a control model can improve the network stability, ensure

an efficient administration of large-scale and heterogeneous networks, and offer load balancing. However, it is difficult to maintain the knowledge of the overall or at least partial state of the network

– Hybrid model: It encompasses both centralized and distributed models. In fact, local controllers are used for local applications to provide the data-path with faster responses for requests that can be handled by a local control application. Only decisions that require centralized network state are redirected to a global controller; this functional behaviour reduces the load at the global controller.

Infrastructure Layer: It is the lower layer of the SDN architecture and is also called data plane. This layer includes physical and/or virtual networking devices, such as routers, physical/virtual switches and access points; equipment may be interconnected via a wired or wireless channel. The data plane in responsible for all data activities including forwarding, fragmentation, and reassembly according to the rules specified by the controller [65,66].

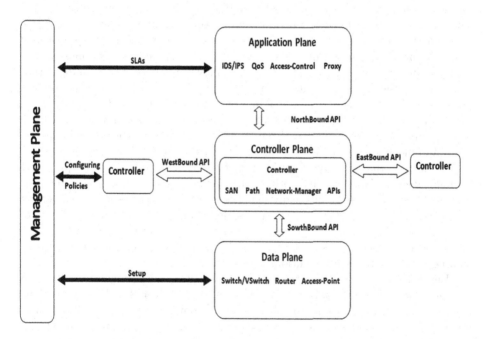

Fig. 2. SDN architecture

As mentioned before, different Application Programming Interfaces (APIs) [10,65] are deployed to ensure communication between SDN architecture's layers, mainly:

- Northbound API: It enables the interaction between the SDN controller and the application layer. It also provides an abstract view of the network to the upper layer.
- Southbound API: It is responsible for interfacing between the control plane and the data plane. The controllers can deploy different rules in the forwarding devices and these devices can communicate with the controller in real-time. OpenFlow is the most common and popular southbound API [68].
- Eastbound/westbound APIs: The eastbound/westbound API allows controllers to communicate among themselves or with other SDN systems to exchange control information regarding the flow in the data plane.

4.2   SDN Use in Smart City Applications

As a complex and multidisciplinary concept, smart cities bring a new set of issues, such as scalability, heterogeneity, interoperability, security and privacy. In fact, with the increasing demand for more sophisticated and complex services, most current solutions are not able to handle these new needs efficiently. In this context, Software Defined Networking can be very useful for a smart city [9]; it has been progressively extending its footsteps in diverse smart city applications such as smart grid, smart mobility, e-health. To carry out these applications, a tremendous number of smart devices are deployed to sense diverse information from the physical environment and to interact with it; this number is growing exponentially generating a huge volume of data of different nature (structured or unstructured). To support the rapid scale-up of sensors and to be able to process and store data collected from these IoT devices, providing scalable systems and mechanisms seems to be necessary for the correct functioning of smart cities. In this context, relying on SDN distributed controllers can be proposed to alleviate the burden on network devices for large-scale applications [63]. For example, with the continuous increase in the number of vehicles and the diversity of Internet of Vehicule (IoV) applications, deploying programmable architecture with a distributed or hybrid model is required to ensure the needs of modern transportation services, as explained in Table 3; however, the size of the network can be a barrier to such a solution.

Besides, throughout a smart city, huge amounts of real-time data, related to citizens, their activities and their location, are shared, stored and analyzed. This ability of smart applications to collect sensitive data raises several security and privacy issues, leading users to express very serious concerns about the safety, accessibility of those services. Many malicious attacks can produce false data or lead to the sale of a large amount of sensitive information about users' private life, which can result in a loss of control of the smart system. For these reasons, it is essential to implement security countermeasures at the different layers of smart city architectures. In this regard, several SDN-based solutions have been proposed to secure different intelligent applications. For example, e-health applications collect and forward sensitive data about the patient status for remote processing and analysis in order to make appropriate diagnostics; unauthorized access and misuse of the patient' health information database can lead to false diagnostics. SDN can enable the integration and the use of different security mechanisms or dispense with different security policies from a specific SDN controller to implement on the network devices, as explained in Table 2. Smart home is another example of applications where security solutions are required to secure home networks and protect collected data through implementing firewalls or network-based intrusion detection mechanisms. Despite the use of SDN in several security solutions, the security of the SDN controller is a challenge.

Being able to simplify the configuration of the growing number of network devices and to integrate new features and technologies to cope with application needs and recent advances is another major challenge for smart city applications. As new technologies emerge and develop, Smart City applications must be scalable, flexible and able to integrate them. This process requires enormous efforts for manual implementation and configuration, which are time consuming and require very high technical skills. To simplify these complex tasks, the programmability and centralized control mechanism of the SDN technology allow network operators to implement and deploy new functionalities and to integrate easily new technologies in a transparent and hardware-independent way. For example, new configuration functionalities for smart home networks can be easily added by simply being programmed at the controller level without interacting with network components, as mentioned in Table 2. In the case of smart grids, to add new measures for detecting communication link failures, they simply need to be implemented at the controller level, which will transmit them in the form of directives to the various smart grid components (see Table 1). In smart cities, different smart devices communicate with each other through different communication networks while applying specific rules during data transfer to meet the requirements of each application and the type of carried data. Generally, manual interventions of network operators are required to reprogram each network device in order to monitor and manage the network and the packet transfer. These management and control tasks become more complex and time consuming depending on the number of involved devices. In this context, SDN technology can be very useful for network management. Indeed, SDN separates the data plane and the network control plane, as network operators are able to program directly the network management rules (addition, deletion, update, etc.) at the controller level without intervening at the hardware level. As a result, network management becomes automatic, simpler and faster. Taking into account specific requirements during configuration step allows improving network responsiveness and service delivery, ensuring a more seamless and better end-user experience.

In addition, SDN users can leverage a view of the entire network through a centralized controller, simplifying consequently provisioning and management processes. For example, as mentioned in Table 1, by integrating SDN into Smart Grid (SG), the SDN controller can modify the packet handling rules in switches in a quick and easy way according to application requirements and network traffic conditions. Similarly, to add new routing rules for the transmission of data packets in VANETs, the network operator intervenes at the controller level to implement them; such control decisions can take into account different criteria, namely the contact duration, the vehicles' speed, the free load, etc. Interoperability problems at the application level often stem also from the perceived heterogeneity in a smart city, which comprises a large and heterogeneous set of smart devices with different functions and from different vendors, communication protocols, network access technologies, etc. Thus, unified standards and an interoperable vendor ecosystem are necessary to support smart city applications. As SDN is hardware-independent and runs on open standards, it has been deployed to facilitate the deployment and configuration of network devices in a transparent and abstract way. For example, in the case of the smart home, the management of heterogeneous communication networks is done transparently and automatically at the controller level.

For many smart city applications, resilience is a major issue in order to guarantee the reliability and security of offered services; a network is resilient if it is able to function normally even in the event of a failure or attack. In the case of e-health monitoring applications, the exchange of information must be timely, reliable and secure in order to be able to react effectively in the case of a patient's condition worsening or an incident. As SDN has proven its ability to ensure rapid recovery and to keep functioning even in the case of equipment failure, power outage or other disruptions, several smart applications have leveraged it to ensure their resilience. The smart grid, among other applications, used SDN for rapid fault detection and recovery.

In the following tables, we present smart city applications which have extensively exploited SDN. For each application, we detail how SDN has been exploited (objectives) and the challenges faced by such SDN based solutions.

Table 1. SDN applied to smart environment applications

Application: Smart Grid
Smart Grid is a system that deploys information and communication technologies on the existing power grid to improve the efficiency of conventional power generation systems by promoting the use of renewable energy. In addition, it consists of distribution networks and intelligent devices dedicated to the collection and analysis of real time data related to the transmission, distribution and consumption of electrical energy, according to energy supply and demand [69, 70]
Objectives
Stability:
– Ensure voltage stability of the electrical network through real-time control and transmission of variable traffic demands between substations [71]
– Ensure smart grid stability (voltage control, supervision and monitoring of injected energy) and address power deficiency [71, 72]
– Ensure load balancing to reduce overload [73]

(contniued)

Table 1. *(contniued)*

Application: Smart Grid
Security: Smart grids are based on complex infrastructures (several numbers of sensors, actuators, smart meters, supervision control,...), they are facing several security issues. To enhance SG security, SDN technology was exploited to detect, mitigate and prevent the security threats in SG systems [74–78]
Network management: As smart grids are heterogeneous, large-scale and distributed over large geographic zones, networking communications and autonomous management and control are challenging tasks. SDN allows to streamline network management and simplify the addition of new functionality through controller programmability and the integration of new technologies [79, 80]
Routing: The number of smart devices is increasing with the deployment of smart grids. As a result, a huge amount of data must be exchanged which can lead to congestion problems. SDN was introduced to bring more reliability to SG traffic through its alternative route selection, route reservation and re-routing capabilities [17, 81]
Challenges
– In SDN, control plane and the data plane communicate through interfaces, using out-of-band network. Such a communication may be expensive and may be infeasible for large network topologies, as it requires a separate dedicated communication link to support control traffic between the controller and the network devices
– Since smart grid is composed of different vendor specific devices and protocols, it is necessary to implement standards to address interoperability issues of smart grid communication (SGC) systems based on the SDN [82]
– Despite its capabilities to secure smart grids, the SDN controller can be vulnerable and susceptible to attacks, especially for the centralized controller case; the recourse to the distributed or hybrid models seems an attractive solution to manage this single point of failure. Furthermore, given the important role of the SDN network hypervisor, it is necessary to secure it in the context of SDN-based SGC [83]
– Being a hot research topic, virtualization through SDNs in the context of the smart grid has been tackled by many recent works, mainly in substations to easily realize dynamic configurations and management cases [84, 85]. However, it is important to take into account the issue of scalability and heterogeneity when designing virtualization protocols for SGCs based on the SDN
– To manage power flows between different SG entities in a reliable and efficient manner, it is important to integrate real-time quality of services (QoS) capability with end-to-end traffic flows in the internet of energy (EI) [86]

Table 2. SDN applied to smart living applications

Application: Smart Home
As mentioned in [87], a smart home is *"a home that incorporates advanced automation systems to provide the inhabitants with sophisticated monitoring and control over the building's functions. For example a smart home may control lighting, temperature, multi-media, security, window and door operations, as well as many other functions."*

Objectives
Security: The increased deployment of Internet-connected smart devices in homes, which collect a variety of sensitive data, raises the vectors of attack and makes it more difficult to ensure privacy and security. In this context, SDN has been widely adopted to secure and manage the smart home network including devices and services efficiently and accurately. For example: – Implement additional security measures in the home network so that network level threats will be identified and blocked [88] – Implement a firewall platform to detect and block horizontal port scans for vulnerable devices [89] – Implement network-based intrusion detection and mitigation solution to protect smart home environments [90]
Autoconfiguration: The growth in the number of heterogeneous connected devices makes home networks more and more complex; therefore, high technical skills are required for their configuration, management and maintenance. To enable the automatic configuration of home networks, several problems related to the heterogeneity of software standards and hardware (gateway, server, ...) must be addressed. In this context, the SDN is proposed as a solution to automatically configure the home network [91]
Heterogeneous network management: Several heterogeneous networks, such as Ethernet, Wi-Fi and power-line communications are involved in data transfer. As there is no automatic optimization between technologies, the choice of transmission technology is made manually. In this context, SDN has been used to manage the heterogeneity of home networks [92]

Challenges
In the context of smart homes, several SDN based solutions have been proposed to tackle different aspects : management, network auto-configuration, security, QoS, etc. These solutions propose different architectures, protocols and prototypes, which are independent of each other. It is essential to propose to propose a unified framework, a kind of single standard for software-defined home networking dealing with all these aspects

Application: e-Health
As mentioned in [93], E-health relies on the use of digital technologies and telecommunications to reduce costs, improve the quality of life and bring improvement in health care services, by reducing clinical errors and keeping track of patient status through better health information, gathered through smart devices (vital signs, activity, etc.)

Objectives
Security: To protect confidential patient health report, the SDN controller analyses network traffic flows to detect security attacks in the cloud environment, where data is generally stored for remote access by authorized persons. Based on the analysis report, it decides whether or not to send confidential data [94]
Ehealth network management: – Address problems related to the huge consumption of network resources and efficient data management [95] – Handle the complexity related to the deployment of an heterogeneous network, efficiently manage connected devices and connections and reduce overload [96] – Control and manage the physical infrastructure and accelerate the innovation of various healthcare applications [97] – Reduce data transmission time through load balancing [98]
Routing: Ensure data transfer while providing more flexibility and reducing energy consumption [99]

Challenges
– Handle heterogeneity and interoperability of diverse types of platforms and servers used in a large-scale health care system, inducing several challenges, such as scalability, connectivity, resource and data management, and reliability of nodes [96] – A health care system involves a huge number of patients and normal persons; related sensitive data is collected, forwarded, processed and stored remotely. In addition to privacy and security concerns, users acquire and own their own medical data through IoT devices,then, patient permission-based authorization is needed for any special configuration or update [94,100]

Table 3. SDN applied to smart mobility

Application: VANETs
Vehicle Ad hoc NETworks (VANETs) allow vehicles and road units (RSUs) to communicate and interact with each other. With advent of IoV, VANETs are rapidly developing around the world. In VANETs, three main modes of communication are possible: Vehicle-to-Vehicle communication (V2V), Vehicle-to-Infrastructure communication (V2I) and hybrid communication. The main objective of deploying VANET is to improve road safety and reduce the number of accidents, while providing comfort to drivers and passengers [47,67]

Objectives
Security:
– Ensure secure communications (thanks to the controller) through the encryption of messages exchanged between vehicles and infrastructures to preserve the confidentiality of V2V and V2I communications [101]
– Provide an authentication process to prevent different types of impersonation attacks at the different network elements [102]
Routing:
– Compute optimized paths for message propagation in VANET while reducing overhead [103]
– Prevent congestion while providing optimal routing routes [104]
Traffic congestion: Detect congestion hotspots in a vehicle network and forecast future congestion in these anticipated hotspots [105]

Challenges
– Develop mechanisms to handle high network mobility management issues (Dynamic network topology, disconnections)
– Improve existing rules and flow policies to meet the essential requirements of new VANET applications
– Protect the controllers of the SDN against various cyber attacks and investigate new security vulnerabilities that may arise as a result of the integration of VANET and SDN or other technologies
– To enable effective communication between these heterogeneous V2X networks, it is necessary to develop efficient interworking mechanisms [15]

In this section, we have examined how SDN has been leveraged by some large-scale smart applications; only a few smart city applications have widely explored the benefits of this paradigm. Thanks to its programmability, SDN has proven its performance in improving network management, routing, configuration, etc. However, it has also shown its limits, mainly in terms of security and scalability [106]. In fact, large-scale applications, such as smart grids, involve widespread networks; network expansion in terms of size and diameter negatively affects network performance in terms of communication delay. For a centralized model, the increase in communication delays between the network devices and the SDN controller induces higher latency, inappropriate for real-time data flows. The distributed control model can ensure network scalability while preserving good performance; to this end, a well-studied strategy is needed to propose a relevant control distribution scheme taking into account the SDN control plane organization and the physical placement of SDN controllers. To ensure a strong consistency when deploying distributed controllers, frequent state updates between network devices and controllers are be required, which may penalize latency. Besides, the central controller failure can lead to the entire network failure. In this case, the use of multiple controllers in a physically distributed (but logically centralized) controller architecture can resolve this problem; however, new issues related to control state redundancy and controller failover may arise [63].

Moreover, SDN security concerns are unexplored; a significant experience on the functioning and use of an SDN system is required in order to acquire enough knowledge to defend an SDN-based system against external threats. In addition, giving users full access to the SDN network may cause internal threats, if the privileges granted are improperly used; even any accidental undesired network manipulation may have negative impact on network performances.

Finally, the lack of open standards for controller-to-controller communications and the heterogeneity of data models used by SDN controller vendors limit interoperability between SDN controller platforms. For this reason, a common data model is needed to achieve interoperability and facilitate standardization tasks in SDNs.

5   Conclusion

For many years, research has been undertaken to leverage the benefits of SDN in many domains and assess the performances of proposed solutions. In this paper, we give an overview of how SDN capabilities have been exploited to sustain smart city applications. Although the integration of SDN in the development of smart city applications has overcome some challenges, mainly scalability, interoperability and security, it remains limited to a few areas: smart environment, smart life, and smart mobility. It is therefore worth exploring and studying the potential benefits of SDN in the other domains of smart cities, i.e. smart economy, smart government, smart people, etc. We also provide an overview of the open issues that need to be addressed. Further research and studies are needed to address such limitations and a substantial learning is required to acquire enough expertise on SDN use to be able to manage such systems and protect them against threats and deficiencies. For example, when dealing with privacy and security issues, SDN was extensively used to tackle such issues. However, as mentioned before, in addition to the lack of open standards, many SDN security concerns are unexplored. Besides, security must be set at all levels of the systems: physical, communication, and processing and storage components. To reinforce security, SDN can be coupled with other concepts, like Blockchain or game theory. To this end, an integrated and holistic approach to address challenges is required.

Only the combined benefits of the various emerging technologies can provide the adequate boost to the achievement of sustainable and safe smart city ecosystems.

References

1. Berzins, K., Greb, H., Young, M.H., Hardee, K.: Urbanization, population, and health myths: addressing common misconceptions with strategic health communication. In: Okigbo, C.C. (ed.) Strategic Urban Health Communication, pp. 25–36. Springer, New York (2014). https://doi.org/10.1007/978-1-4614-9335-8_3
2. Sanchez-Corcuera, R., et al.: Smart cities survey: technologies, application domains and challenges for the cities of the future. Int. J. Distrib. Sensor Netw. **15**(6), 1550147719853984 (2019)
3. Pellicer, S., Santa, G., Bleda, A.L., Maestre, R., Jara, A.J., Skarmeta, A.G.: A global perspective of smart cities: a survey. In: 2013 Seventh International Conference on Innovative Mobile and Internet Services in Ubiquitous Computing, pp. 439–444. IEEE, July 2013
4. Kim, T.H., Ramos, C., Mohammed, S.: Smart city and IoT (2017)
5. Yin, C., Xiong, Z., Chen, H., Wang, J., Cooper, D., David, B.: A literature survey on smart cities. Sci. China Inf. Sci. **58**(10), 1–18 (2015)
6. Zhang, K., Ni, J., Yang, K., Liang, X., Ren, J., Shen, X.S.: Security and privacy in smart city applications: challenges and solutions. IEEE Commun. Mag. **55**(1), 122–129 (2017)
7. Silva, B.N., Khan, M., Han, K.: Towards sustainable smart cities: a review of trends, architectures, components, and open challenges in smart cities. Sustain. Cities Soc. **38**, 697–713 (2018)
8. Okai, E., Feng, X., Sant, P.: Smart cities survey. In: IEEE 20th International Conference on High Performance Computing and Communications; IEEE 16th International Conference on Smart City; IEEE 4th International Conference on Data Science and Systems (HPCC/SmartCity/DSS), pp. 1726–1730. IEEE, June 2018
9. Martins, J.S.: Towards smart city innovation under the perspective of software-defined networking, artificial intelligence and big data (2018). arXiv preprint arXiv:1810.11665
10. Kreutz, D., Ramos, F.M., Verissimo, P.E., Rothenberg, C.E., Azodolmolky, S., Uhlig, S.: Software-defined networking: a comprehensive survey. Proc. IEEE **103**(1), 14–76 (2014)
11. Nunes, B.A.A., Mendonca, M., Nguyen, X.N., Obraczka, K., Turletti, T.: A survey of software-defined networking: past, present, and future of programmable networks. IEEE Commun. Surv. Tutor. **16**(3), 1617–1634 (2014)
12. da Rocha Fonseca, P.C., Mota, E.S.: A survey on fault management in software-defined networks. IEEE Commun. Surv. Tutor. **19**(4), 2284–2321 (2017)
13. Khan, S., Gani, A., Wahab, A.W.A., Guizani, M., Khan, M.K.: Topology discovery in software defined networks: threats, taxonomy, and state-of-the-art. IEEE Commun. Surv. Tutor. **19**(1), 303–324 (2016)
14. Guck, J.W., Van Bemten, A., Reisslein, M., Kellerer, W.: Unicast QoS routing algorithms for SDN: a comprehensive survey and performance evaluation. IEEE Commun. Surv. Tutor. **20**(1), 388–415 (2017)
15. Jaballah, W.B., Conti, M., Lal, C.: A survey on software-defined VANETs: benefits, challenges, and future directions (2019). arXiv preprint arXiv:1904.04577

16. Chahal, M., Harit, S., Mishra, K.K., Sangaiah, A.K., Zheng, Z.: A survey on software-defined networking in vehicular ad hoc networks: challenges, applications and use cases. Sustain. Cities Soc. **35**, 830–840 (2017)

17. Rehmani, M.H., Davy, A., Jennings, B., Assi, C.: Software defined networks-based smart grid communication: a comprehensive survey. IEEE Commun. Surv. Tutor. **21**(3), 2637–2670 (2019)

18. Alshnta, A.M., Abdollah, M.F., Al-Haiqi, A.: SDN in the home: a survey of home network solutions using software defined networking. Cogent Eng. **5**(1), 1469949 (2018)

19. Harrison, C., et al.: Foundations for smarter cities. IBM J. Res. Dev. **54**(4), 1–16 (2010)

20. Marsal-Llacuna, M.L., Colomer-Llinàs, J., Meléndez-Frigola, J.: Lessons in urban monitoring taken from sustainable and livable cities to better address the smart cities initiative. Technol. Forecast. Soc. Change **90**, 611–622 (2015)

21. Praharaj, S., Han, H.: Cutting through the clutter of smart city definitions: a reading into the smart city perceptions in India. City Cult. Soc. **18**, 100289 (2019)

22. Neirotti, P., De Marco, A., Cagliano, A.C., Mangano, G., Scorrano, F.: Current trends in smart city initiatives: some stylised facts. Cities **38**, 25–36 (2014)

23. Al-Turjman, F., Zahmatkesh, H., Shahroze, R.: An overview of security and privacy in smart cities' IoT communications. Trans. Emerg. Telecomm. Technol. e3677 (2019)

24. Schaffers, H., Ratti, C., Komninos, N.: Special issue on smart applications for smart cities-new approaches to innovation: guest editors' introduction. J. Theoret. Appl. Electron. Commer. Res. **7**(3), 2–5 (2012)

25. Giffinger, R., Fertner, C., Kramar, H., Kalasek, R., Pichler-Milanovic, N., Meijers, E.: Smart Cities: Ranking of European medium-sized cities. Centre of Regional Science (SRF), Vienna, Austria (2007)

26. Albino, V., Berardi, U., Dangelico, R.M.: Smart cities: definitions, dimensions, performance, and initiatives. J. Urban Technol. **22**(1), 3–21 (2015)

27. Winters, J.V.: Why are smart cities growing? Who moves and who stays. J. Reg. Sci. **51**(2), 253–270 (2011)

28. Nam, T., Pardo, T.A.: Conceptualizing smart city with dimensions of technology, people, and institutions. In: Proceedings of the 12th Annual International Digital Government Research Conference: Digital Government Innovation in Challenging Times, pp. 282–291, June 2011

29. Giffinger, R., Gudrun, H.: Smart cities ranking: an effective instrument for the positioning of the cities? ACE Archit. City Environ. **4**(12), 7–26 (2010)

30. Zubizarreta, I., Seravalli, A., Arrizabalaga, S.: Smart city concept: what it is and what it should be. J. Urban Plann. Develop. **142**(1), 04015005 (2016)

31. Laohajaratsang, T.: e-Education in Thailand: equity, quality and sensitivity for learners and teachers. In: Global Learn, pp. 694–700. Association for the Advancement of Computing in Education (AACE), May 2010

32. Pereira, G.V., Parycek, P., Falco, E., Kleinhans, R.: Smart governance in the context of smart cities: a literature review. Inf. Polity **23**(2), 143–162 (2018)

33. Twizeyimana, J.D., Andersson, A.: The public value of e-government-a literature review. Govern. Inf. Q. **36**(2), 167–178 (2019)

34. Lindner, R., Aichholzer, G.: E-democracy: conceptual foundations and recent trends. In: Hennen, L., van Keulen, I., Korthagen, I., Aichholzer, G., Lindner, R., Nielsen, R.Ø. (eds.) European E-Democracy in Practice. SDPG, pp. 11–45. Springer, Cham (2020). https://doi.org/10.1007/978-3-030-27184-8_2

35. Chetouane, A., Mabrouk, S., Jemili, I., Mosbah, M.: A comparative study of vehicle detection methods in a video sequence. In: Jemili, I., Mosbah, M. (eds.) DiCES-N 2019. CCIS, vol. 1130, pp. 37–53. Springer, Cham (2020). https://doi.org/10.1007/978-3-030-40131-3_3

36. Chetouane, A., Mabrouk, S., Jemili, I., Mosbah, M.: Vision-based vehicle detection for road traffic congestion classification. Concurr. Comput. Pract. Exp. e5983 (2020)

37. Abdallah, A., Jemili, I., Mabrouk, S., Mosbah, M.: Leveraging GPS data for vehicle maneuver detection. In: International Workshop on Communication Technologies for Vehicles. Springer, Cham (2020)

38. Ahmed, E., Yaqoob, I., Gani, A., Imran, M., Guizani, M.: Internet-of-things-based smart environments: state of the art, taxonomy, and open research challenges. IEEE Wirel. Commun. **23**(5), 10–16 (2016)

39. Dileep, G.: A survey on smart grid technologies and applications. Renewab. Energy **146**, 2589–2625 (2020)

40. Chew, I., Karunatilaka, D., Tan, C.P., Kalavally, V.: Smart lighting: the way forward? Reviewing the past to shape the future. Energy and Build. **149**, 180–191 (2017)

41. Negra, R., Jemili, I., Belghith, A., Mosbah, M.: MTM-MAC: medical traffic management mac protocol for handling healthcare applications in WBANs. In: Palattella, M.R., Scanzio, S., Coleri Ergen, S. (eds.) ADHOC-NOW 2019. LNCS, vol. 11803, pp. 483–497. Springer, Cham (2019). https://doi.org/10.1007/978-3-030-31831-4_33

42. Negra, R., Jemili, I., Belghith, A.: Wireless body area networks: applications and technologies. Procedia Comput. Sci. **83**, 1274–1281 (2016)

43. Negra, R., Jemili, I., Zemmari, A., Mosbah, M., Belghith, A.: WBAN path loss based approach for human activity recognition with machine learning techniques. In: 14th International Wireless Communications & Mobile Computing Conference (IWCMC), pp. 470–475. IEEE, June 2018

44. Hargreaves, T., Wilson, C., Hauxwell-Baldwin, R.: Learning to live in a smart home. Build. Res. Inf. **46**(1), 127–139 (2018)

45. Alaa, M., Zaidan, A.A., Zaidan, B.B., Talal, M., Kiah, M.L.M.: A review of smart home applications based on Internet of Things. J. Netw. Comput. Appl. **97**, 48–65 (2017)

46. Sookhak, M., Tang, H., He, Y., Yu, F.R.: Security and privacy of smart cities: a survey, research issues and challenges. IEEE Commun. Surv. Tutor. **21**(2), 1718–1743 (2018)

47. Ksouri, C., Jemili, I., Mosbah, M., Belghith, A.: Data gathering for Internet of vehicles safety. In: 2018 14th International Wireless Communications & Mobile Computing Conference (IWCMC), pp. 904–909. IEEE, June 2018

48. Capponi, A., Fiandrino, C., Kantarci, B., Foschini, L., Kliazovich, D., Bouvry, P.: A survey on mobile crowdsensing systems: challenges, solutions, and opportunities. IEEE Commun. Surv. Tutor. **21**(3), 2419–2465 (2019)

49. Cui, L., Xie, G., Qu, Y., Gao, L., Yang, Y.: Security and privacy in smart cities: challenges and opportunities. IEEE Access **6**, 46134–46145 (2018)

50. Balakrishna, C.: Enabling technologies for smart city services and applications. In: Sixth International Conference on Next Generation Mobile Applications, Services and Technologies, pp. 223–227. IEEE, September 2012

51. Habibzadeh, H., Nussbaum, B.H., Anjomshoa, F., Kantarci, B., Soyata, T.: A survey on cybersecurity, data privacy, and policy issues in cyber-physical system deployments in smart cities. Sustain. Cities Soc. **50**, 101660 (2019)

52. Kazmi, A., Jan, Z., Zappa, A., Serrano, M.: Overcoming the heterogeneity in the internet of things for smart cities. In: Podnar Žarko, I., Broering, A., Soursos, S., Serrano, M. (eds.) InterOSS-IoT 2016. LNCS, vol. 10218, pp. 20–35. Springer, Cham (2017). https://doi.org/10.1007/978-3-319-56877-5_2

53. Mehmood, Y., Ahmad, F., Yaqoob, I., Adnane, A., Imran, M., Guizani, S.: Internet-of-things-based smart cities: recent advances and challenges. IEEE Commun. Mag. **55**(9), 16–24 (2017)

54. Gharaibeh, A., et al.: Smart cities: a survey on data management, security, and enabling technologies. IEEE Commun. Surv. Tutor. **19**(4), 2456–2501 (2017)

55. Khalid, A.: Smart applications for smart live. Int. J. Comput. Sci. Mob. Comput. **5**, 97–103 (2016)

56. Pasolini, G., et al.: Smart city pilot projects using LoRa and IEEE802.15.4 technologies. Sensors **18**(4), 1118 (2018)

57. Yaqoob, I., Hashem, I.A.T., Mehmood, Y., Gani, A., Mokhtar, S., Guizani, S.: Enabling communication technologies for smart cities. IEEE Commun. Mag. **55**(1), 112–120 (2017)

58. Chourabi, H., et al.: Understanding smart cities: an integrative framework. In: 45th Hawaii International Conference on System Sciences, pp. 2289–2297. IEEE, January 2012

59. Santana, E.F.Z., Chaves, A.P., Gerosa, M.A., Kon, F., Milojicic, D.S.: Software platforms for smart cities: concepts, requirements, challenges, and a unified reference architecture. ACM Comput. Surv. (CSUR) **50**(6), 1–37 (2017)

60. Oussous, A., Benjelloun, F.Z., Lahcen, A.A., Belfkih, S.: Big data technologies: a survey. J. King Saud Univ. Comput. Inf. Sci. **30**(4), 431–448 (2018)

61. Lu, G., Zeng, W.H.: Cloud computing survey. In Applied Mechanics and Materials, vol. 530, pp. 650–661. Trans Tech Publications Ltd. (2014)

62. Atzori, L., Iera, A., Morabito, G.: The internet of things: a survey. Comput. Netw. **54**(15), 2787–2805 (2010)

63. Bannour, F., Souihi, S., Mellouk, A.: Distributed SDN control: survey, taxonomy, and challenges. IEEE Commun. Surv. Tutor. **20**(1), 333–354 (2018)

64. Kim, H., Feamster, N.: Improving network management with software defined networking. IEEE Commun. Mag. **51**(2), 114–119 (2013)

65. Zemrane, H., Baddi, Y., Hasbi, A.: SDN-based solutions to improve IoT: survey. In: IEEE 5th International Congress on Information Science and Technology (CiSt), pp. 588–593. IEEE, October 2018

66. Neghabi, A.A., Navimipour, N.J., Hosseinzadeh, M., Rezaee, A.: Load balancing mechanisms in the software defined networks: a systematic and comprehensive review of the literature. IEEE Access **6**, 14159–14178 (2018)

67. Alouache, L., Nguyen, N., Aliouat, M., Chelouah, R.: Survey on IoV routing protocols: security and network architecture. Int. J. Commun. Syst. **32**(2), e3849 (2019)

68. Alsaeedi, M., Mohamad, M.M., Al-Roubaiey, A.A.: Toward adaptive and scalable OpenFlow-SDN flow control: a survey. IEEE Access **7**, 107346–107379 (2019)

69. Fang, X., Misra, S., Xue, G., Yang, D.: Smart grid-the new and improved power grid: a survey. IEEE Commun. Surv. Tutor. **14**(4), 944–980 (2011)

70. Kim, J., Filali, F., Ko, Y.B.: Trends and potentials of the smart grid infrastructure: from ICT sub-system to SDN-enabled smart grid architecture. Appl. Sci. **5**(4), 706–727 (2015)

71. Dorsch, N., Kurtz, F., Dalhues, S., Robitzky, L., Häger, U., Wietfeld, C.: Intertwined: Software-defined communication networks for multi-agent system-based smart grid control. In: IEEE International Conference on Smart Grid Communications (SmartGridComm), pp. 254–259. IEEE, November 2016

72. Rayati, M., Ranjbar, A.: Resilient transactive control for systems with high wind penetration based on cloud computing. IEEE Trans. Ind. Inf. **14**(3), 1286–1296 (2018)

73. Hannon, C., Yan, J., Jin, D.: DSSnet: a smart grid modeling platform combining electrical power distribution system simulation and software defined networking emulation. In: Proceedings of the ACM SIGSIM Conference Principles Advanced Discrete Simulation (SIGSIM-PADS), pp. 131–142 (2016)

74. Jin, D.: Toward a cyber resilient and secure microgrid using software-defined networking. IEEE Trans. Smart Grid **8**(5), 2494–2504 (2017)

75. Chaudhary, R., Aujla, G.S., Garg, S., Kumar, N., Rodrigues, J.J.: SDN-enabled multi-attribute-based secure communication for smart grid in IIoT environment. IEEE Trans. Ind. Inf. **14**(6), 2629–2640 (2018)

76. Demirci, S., Sagiroglu, S.: Software-defined networking for improving security in smart grid systems. In: 7th International Conference on Renewable Energy Research and Applications (ICRERA), pp. 1021–1026. IEEE, October 2018

77. Ibdah, D., Kanani, M., Lachtar, N., Allan, N., Al-Duwairi, B.: On the security of SDN-enabled smartgrid systems. In: International Conference on Electrical and Computing Technologies and Applications (ICECTA), pp. 1–5. IEEE, November 2017

78. Ghosh, U., Chatterjee, P., Shetty, S.: A security framework for SDN-enabled smart power grids. In: IEEE 37th International Conference on Distributed Computing Systems Workshops (ICDCSW), pp. 113–118. IEEE, June 2017

79. Rinaldi, S., Ferrari, P., Brandão, D., Sulis, S.: Software defined networking applied to the heterogeneous infrastructure of smart grid. In: IEEE World Conference on Factory Communication Systems (WFCS), pp. 1–4. IEEE, May 2015

80. Molina, E., Jacob, E., Matias, J., Moreira, N., Astarloa, A.: Using software defined networking to manage and control IEC 61850-based systems. Comput. Electric. Eng. **43**, 142–154 (2015)

81. Pfeiffenberger, T., Du, J.L., Arruda, P.B., Anzaloni, A.: Reliable and flexible communications for power systems: fault-tolerant multicast with SDN/OpenFlow. In: 7th International Conference on New Technologies, Mobility and Security (NTMS), pp. 1–6. IEEE, July 2015

82. Chang, K.H.: Interoperable nan standards: a path to cost-effective smart grid solutions. IEEE Wirel. Commun. **20**(3), 4–5 (2013)

83. Ali, S.T., Sivaraman, V., Radford, A., Jha, S.: A survey of securing networks using software defined networking. IEEE Trans. Reliab. **64**(3), 1086–1097 (2015)

84. Dorsch, N., Jablkowski, B., Georg, H., Spinczyk, O., Wietfeld, C.: Analysis of communication networks for smart substations using a virtualized execution platform. In: IEEE International Conference on Communications (ICC), pp. 4239–4245. IEEE, June 2014

85. Kurtz, F., Bektas, C., Dorsch, N., Wietfeld, C.: Network slicing for critical communications in shared 5G infrastructures-an empirical evaluation. In: 4th IEEE Conference on Network Softwarization and Workshops (NetSoft), pp. 393–399. IEEE, June 2018

86. Bui, N., Castellani, A.P., Casari, P., Zorzi, M.: The internet of energy: a web-enabled smart grid system. IEEE Network **26**(4), 39–45 (2012)

87. Smart Home Energy. http://smarthomeenergy.co.uk. Accessed 06 Oct 2020
88. Sivaraman, V., Gharakheili, H.H., Vishwanath, A., Boreli, R., Mehani, O.: Network-level security and privacy control for smart-home IoT devices. In: IEEE 11th International Conference on Wireless and Mobile Computing, Networking and Communications (WiMob), pp. 163–167. IEEE, October 2015
89. Shirali-Shahreza, S., Ganjali, Y.: Protecting home user devices with an SDN-based firewall. IEEE Trans. Consum. Electron. **64**(1), 92–100 (2018)
90. Nobakht, M., Sivaraman, V., Boreli, R.: A host-based intrusion detection and mitigation framework for smart home IoT using OpenFlow. In: 11th International Conference on Availability, Reliability and Security (ARES), pp. 147–156. IEEE, August 2016
91. Lee, M., Kim, Y., Lee, Y.: A home cloud-based home network auto-configuration using SDN. In: IEEE 12th International Conference on Networking, Sensing and Control, pp. 444–449. IEEE, April 2015
92. Soetens, N., Famaey, J., Verstappen, M., Latre, S.: SDN-based management of heterogeneous home networks. In: 11th International Conference on Network and Service Management (CNSM), pp. 402–405. IEEE, November 2015
93. Britannica. https://www.britannica.com. Accessed 07 Oct 2020
94. Srilakshmi, A., Mohanapriya, P., Harini, D., Geetha, K.: IoT based smart health care system to prevent security attacks in SDN. In: 2019 Fifth International Conference on Electrical Energy Systems (ICEES), pp. 1–7. IEEE, February 2019
95. Zemrane, H., Baddi, Y., Hasbi, A.: Improve IoT ehealth ecosystem with SDN. In: Proceedings of the 4th International Conference on Smart City Applications, pp. 1–8, October 2019
96. Sallabi, F., Naeem, F., Awad, M., Shuaib, K.: Managing IoT-based smart healthcare systems traffic with software defined networks. In: International Symposium on Networks, Computers and Communications (ISNCC), pp. 1–6. IEEE, June 2018
97. Hu, L., Qiu, M., Song, J., Hossain, M.S., Ghoneim, A.: Software defined healthcare networks. IEEE Wirel. Commun. **22**(6), 67–75 (2015)
98. Li, T.M., Liao, C.C., Cho, H.H., Chien, W.C., Lai, C.F., Chao, H.C.: An e-healthcare sensor network load-balancing scheme using SDN-SFC. In: IEEE 19th International Conference on e-Health Networking, Applications and Services (Healthcom), pp. 1–4. IEEE, October 2017
99. Cicioğlu, M., Çalhan, A.: SDN-based wireless body area network routing algorithm for healthcare architecture. ETRI J. **41**(4), 452–464 (2019)
100. Hartmann, M., Hashmi, U.S., Imran, A.: Edge computing in smart health care systems: review, challenges, and research directions. Trans. Emerg. Telecomm. Tech. e3710 (2019)
101. Arif, M., Wang, G., Wang, T., Peng, T.: SDN-based secure VANETs communication with fog computing. In: Wang, G., Chen, J., Yang, L.T. (eds.) SpaCCS 2018. LNCS, vol. 11342, pp. 46–59. Springer, Cham (2018). https://doi.org/10.1007/978-3-030-05345-1_4
102. Hussein, A., Elhajj, I. H., Chehab, A., Kayssi, A.: SDN VANETs in 5G: an architecture for resilient security services. In 2017 Fourth International Conference on Software Defined Systems (SDS), pp. 67–74. IEEE, May 2017
103. Zhu, M., Cao, J., Pang, D., He, Z., Xu, M.: SDN-based routing for efficient message propagation in VANET. In: Xu, K., Zhu, H. (eds.) WASA 2015. LNCS, vol. 9204, pp. 788–797. Springer, Cham (2015). https://doi.org/10.1007/978-3-319-21837-3_77

104. Ji, X., Yu, H., Fan, G., Fu, W.: SDGR: an SDN-based geographic routing protocol for VANET. In: IEEE International Conference on Internet of Things (iThings) and IEEE Green Computing and Communications (GreenCom) and IEEE Cyber, Physical and Social Computing (CPSCom) and IEEE Smart Data (SmartData), pp. 276–281. IEEE, December 2016

105. Bhatia, J., Dave, R., Bhayani, H., Tanwar, S., Nayyar, A.: SDN-based real-time urban traffic analysis in VANET environment. Comput. Commun. **149**, 162–175 (2020)

106. Benzekki, K., El Fergougui, A., Elbelrhiti Elalaoui, A.: Software-defined networking (SDN): a survey. Secur. Commun. Netw. **9**(18), 5803–5833 (2016)

Artificial Intelligence and Internet of Things

Dairy Cow Rumination Detection: A Deep Learning Approach

Safa Ayadi[1,2(✉)], Ahmed Ben Said[1,3], Rateb Jabbar[1,3], Chafik Aloulou[2], Achraf Chabbouh[1], and Ahmed Ben Achballah[1]

[1] LifeEye LLC, Tunis, Tunisia
{safa.ayadi,ahmedbs,rateb,achraf,ahmed}@lifeye.io
[2] Faculty of Economics and Management of Sfax,
University of Sfax, 3018 Sfax, Tunisia
chafik.aloulou@fsegs.rnu.tn
[3] Department of Computer Science and Engineering, Qatar University, Doha, Qatar
{abensaid,rateb.jabbar}@qu.edu.qa
https://www.lifeye.io/

Abstract. Cattle activity is an essential index for monitoring health and welfare of the ruminants. Thus, changes in the livestock behavior are a critical indicator for early detection and prevention of several diseases. Rumination behavior is a significant variable for tracking the development and yield of animal husbandry. Therefore, various monitoring methods and measurement equipment have been used to assess cattle behavior. However, these modern attached devices are invasive, stressful and uncomfortable for the cattle and can influence negatively the welfare and diurnal behavior of the animal. Multiple research efforts addressed the problem of rumination detection by adopting new methods by relying on visual features. However, they only use few postures of the dairy cow to recognize the rumination or feeding behavior. In this study, we introduce an innovative monitoring method using Convolution Neural Network (CNN)-based deep learning models. The classification process is conducted under two main labels: ruminating and other, using all cow postures captured by the monitoring camera. Our proposed system is simple and easy-to-use which is able to capture long-term dynamics using a compacted representation of a video in a single 2D image. This method proved efficiency in recognizing the rumination behavior with 95%, 98% and 98% of average accuracy, recall and precision, respectively.

Keywords: Rumination behavior · Dairy cows · Deep learning · Action recognition · Machine learning · Computer vision

1 Introduction

Cattle products are among the most consumed products worldwide (i.e., meat and milk) [1], which makes dairy farmers pressured by the intensity of commercial farming demands to optimize the operational efficiency of the yield system.

© Springer Nature Switzerland AG 2020
I. Jemili and M. Mosbah (Eds.): DiCES-N 2020, CCIS 1348, pp. 123–139, 2020.
https://doi.org/10.1007/978-3-030-65810-6_7

Therefore, maintaining cattle physiological status is an important task to maintain an optimal milk production. It is widely known that rumination behavior is a key indicator for monitoring health and welfare of ruminants [2,3]. When the cow is stressed [4], anxious [5], suffering from severe disease or influenced by any several factors, including the nutrition diet program [6,7], the rumination time will decrease accordingly. Early detection of any abnormality will prevent severe outcomes of the lactation program. Furthermore, the saliva produced while masticating aids to improve the rumen state [8]. Rumination time helps farmers to predict estrus [9] and calving [10,11] period of dairy cows. It was proved that the rumination time reduces on the 14th and 7th day before calving [10] and decreases slowly three days before estrus [9]. By predicting calving moments, the farmer/veterinarian would be able to maintain the health condition of the cow and prevent risks of any disease (e.g., Calf pneumonia) that could be mortal when the cow is having a difficult calving [11].

In previous decades, farmers performed a direct observation to monitor rumination [12]. However, this method has shown many limitations; it is time-consuming and requires labor wages, especially on large-sized farms. In modern farms, many devices based on sensors have been used to automatically monitor animal behavior such as sound sensors [13], noseband pressure sensors [14] and motion sensors [15,16]. However, many of these sensors are designed to extract only a few behavioral patterns (e.g., sound waves), which developed the need of devising an automated system as a mean to assess health and welfare of animals and reduce operational costs for farmers. Machine Learning is able to extract and learn automatically from large-scale data using for example sophisticated Neural Networks (NNs). NNs are mainly used in Deep Learning algorithms that handily become state-of-the-art across a range of difficult problem domains [17–20]. Thus, the use of these developed technologies can improve the monitoring process and achieve an efficient performance in recognizing animal behavior. One of the most common used type of Deep Neural Networks for visual motion recognition is the convolutional neural networks (CNNs). CNNs can automatically recognize deep features from images and accurately perform computer vision tasks [21,22]. Aside from these continuous achievements, these technologies require further improvement due to their lack of precision.

This work proposes a monitoring method to recognize cow rumination behavior. We show that CNN can accurately perform an excellent classification performance using an easy-to-use extension of state-of-the-art base architectures. Our contributions are as follow:

- We propose a simple and easy-to-use method that can capture long-term dynamics through a standard 2D image using dynamic images method [23].
- With a standard deep learning CNN-based model, we accurately performed the classification tasks using all postures of the cows.
- We conduct comprehensive comparative study to validate the effectiveness of the proposed methodology for cow rumination detection.

The remainder of this paper is organized as follows. The related works of this study are presented in Sect. 2. The developed method and the used equipment are described in detail in Sect. 3. The implementation of the model, the evaluation of the yielded results and the comparison with the state-of-the-art are discussed in Sect. 4. Finally, a conclusion and directions for future research are presented in Sect. 5.

2   Related Works

In this section, we review existing research works, equipment and methods that addressed the challenging problem of rumination detection. The existing intelligent monitoring equipment can be split into four categories.

2.1   Sound Sensor for Rumination Detection

The monitoring method with sound sensor, is mainly used to identify the rumination behavior by planting a microphone around the throat, forehead or other parts of the ruminant to record chewing, swallowing or regurgitating behavior. In fact, acoustic methods exhibit excellent performance in recognizing ingestive events. Milone et al. [24] created an automated system to identify ingestive events based on hidden Markov models. The classification of chew and bite had an accuracy of 89% and 58% respectively. Chelotti et al. [25] proposed a Chewbit Intelligent Algorithm (CBIA) using sound sensor and six machine learning algorithms to identify three jaw movement events. This classification achieved 90% recognition performance using the Multi-Layer Perceptron. Clapham et al. [26] used manual identification and sound metrics to identify the jaw movement that detected 95% of behavior, however this system requires manual calibration periodically which is not recommended for automated learning systems. Furthermore, some systems use sound sensors to recognize the rumination and grazing behavior after analysing jaw movement [27,28]. The monitoring methods with sound sensor gave a good performance. However, owing to their high-cost and trends in the distributed signals that negatively affect event detection, these devices are primarily used for research purposes.

2.2   Noseband Pressure Sensor for Rumination Detection

The monitoring method with a noseband pressure sensor, generally used to recognize rumination and feeding behavior using a halter and a data logger to record mastication through picks of pressure. Shen et al. [14] used noseband pressure as core device to monitor the number of ruminations, the duration of rumination and the number of regurgitated bolus and achieved 100%, 94, 2% and 94.45% respectively as results of recognition. Zehner et al. [29] created two software to classify and identify the rumination and eating behavior using two versions of RumiWatch[1] noseband pressure sensors. The achieved detection accuracy 96% and 91% of rumination time and 86% and 96% of feeding time for 1 h resolution

---

[1] https://www.rumiwatch.ch/.

data provided by two noseband devices. The obtained results are important with these technologies however; the monitoring process is only useful for short-term monitoring and requires improvements to efficiently monitor the health and the welfare of animals.

2.3 Triaxial Acceleration Sensor for Rumination Detection

The monitoring method with a triaxial acceleration sensor that can, recognize broader sets of movement at various scales of rotation. It is common to use accelerometer sensors for its low cost. Shen et al. [16] used triaxial accelera-tion to collect jaw movement and classify them into three categories: feeding, ruminating and other using three machine learning algorithms. Among them, the K-Nearest Neighbour (KNN) algorithm scored the best performance with 93.7% of precision. Another work focused on identifying different activities of the cow using Multi-class SVM and the overall model performed 78% of pre-cision and 69% of kappa [30]. Rayas-Amor et al. [31] used the HOBO-Pendant G-three-axis data recorder to monitor grazing and rumination behavior. The sys-tem recognized 96% and 94.5% respectively of 20 variances in visual observation per cow/day. The motion-sensitive bolus sensor was applied by Andrew et al. [32] to measure jaw motion through the bolus movement using SVM algorithm. This algorithm managed to recognize 86% of motion. According to these find-ings, the accelerometer made an interesting performance in recognizing behavior; however, it still confuses activities of animals that share the same postures.

2.4 Video Equipment Sensor for Rumination Detection

The monitoring method with video equipment, recognize ruminant behavior by recording cow movement and extracting visual motions to identify and classify the animal behavior. According to the state-of-the-art, many initiatives focused on detecting the mouth movement using the optical flow technique that can detect motion from two consecutive frames. Mao et al. [15] used this technique to track the rumination behavior of dairy cows automatically. This method reached 87.80% of accuracy. Another work by Li et al. [33] on tracking multiple targets of cows to detect their mouth areas using optical flow technique achieved 89.12% of the tracking rate. The mean shift [34] and STC algorithms [35] were used by Chen et al. [36,37] to monitor the rumination time using the optical flow technique to track the mouth movement of the cow. The monitoring process achieved 92.03% and 85.45% of accuracy, respectively. However, the learning process of these two methods is based only on the prone position and thus, it is not possible to monitor the diurnal rumination behavior in its different pas-tures. On other hand, the mouth tracking method can easily be influenced by cow movement which creates inferences in the training stage. CNN is another technique to extract features from images without any manual extraction. This technology is generally used for object detection [38] and visual action recogni-tion [37,39]. D Li et al. [39] used KELM [40] to identify mounting behavior of pigs. This network achieved approximately 94.5% of accuracy. Yang et al. [41]

applied Faster R-CNN [42] to recognize feeding behavior of group-housed pigs. The algorithm achieved 99.6% of precision and 86.93% of recall. Another recent work based on CNN was proposed by Belkadi et al. [38]. It was developed on commercial dairy cows to recognize the feeding behavior, feeding place and food type. They implemented four CNN-based models to: detect the dairy cow, check availability of the food in the feeder and identify the food category, recognize the feeding behavior and identify each cow. This system is able to detect 92%, 100% and 97% of the feeding state, food type and cow identity, respectively. Although the achieved performance is significant, this method is not suitable for detecting other behaviors since their used images focus only on the feeder area which boosted their performance. Overall, many of these proposed methods worked only with few postures of dairy cows to recognize the rumination or feeding behaviors. Conversely, video analysis methods can easily be influenced by weather conditions and other external, factors which causes noisy effects for the learning performance. These methods are more applicable to monitor cows housed indoors or for commercial purposes [43].

2.5   Evaluation

All the four categories performed well when it comes to recognizing animal behavior. However, many of these wearable devices are invasive, stressful and, accordingly, can influence the diurnal behavior of animals [44]. Thus, using video equipment is more reliable and less invasive. In this work, we propose a method that relies on a non-stressful device and use a deep learning CNN-based method to recognize the rumination behavior of indoor-housed cows automatically.

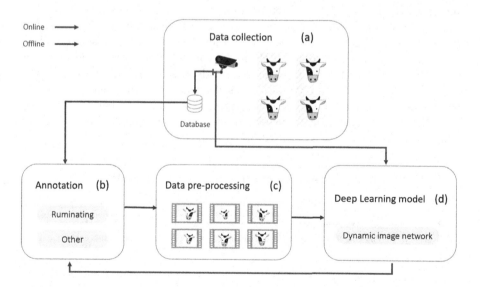

Fig. 1. The proposed system for cow rumination behavior recognition.

3   Method and Materials

Our proposed system, is mainly constructed with four stages as depicted in Fig. 1. We use video equipment as a core device to collect cattle activities. The recorded videos, are continuously stored in the database and automatically segmented into frames. We collect data and carefully annotate it under two main labels (Sect. 3.1). Subsequently, these frames are cleaned from noisy effects and significantly generated to obtain a compacted representation of a video (Sect. 3.2). We apply the dynamic images approach that uses a standard 2D image as input to recognize dairy cow behavior (Sect. 3.3). This method can use a standard CNN-based architecture. All these processes were conducted offline. To implement and test our model, we choose several key architectures (Sect. 3.4) that gave relevant results in the classification stage. To avoid the overfitting of the model, we implemented a few regularization methods that can boost the performance of the network (Sect. 3.5).

3.1   Data Acquisition

The research and experiments were conducted at the Lifeye LLC company[2] for its project entitled Moome[3], based in Tunis (Tunisia). The experimental subjects are Holstein dairy cows farmed indoor originating from different farms of rural areas from the south of Tunisia. Cattles were monitored by cameras planted in a corner offering a complete view of the cow body. The recorded videos were stored in an SD card, then, they were manually fed in the database storage and automatically divided into frames and displayed in the platform. To ensure a real-time monitoring, cameras are directly connected to the developed system. The collected data includes 25,400 frames collected during the daytime and the unlit time in July 2019 and February 2020, then they were accurately distributed into two main labels according to each data folder content. Each data folder contains approximately 243 and 233 frames for 1 min video with a resolution of 640×480 pixels. Figure 3 illustrates examples of used frames. In fact, all captured cow postures were used for the training and testing sets, including, eating, standing, sitting, drinking, ruminating, lifting head and other movements. The definition of dairy cow rumination is presented in Table 1.

Table 1. Definition of dairy cow rumination labels.

Behavior	Definition
Ruminating	The cow is masticating or swallowing of ingesta while sitting or standing
Other	The cow is standing, eating, drinking, sitting or doing any other activity

---

[2] https://www.crunchbase.com/organization/lifeye.
[3] https://www.moome.io.

3.2   Data Pre-processing

The aim of data pre-processing is to improve quality the frames by enhancing important image features or suppressing unwanted distortions from the image. In this study, the methods used for image pre-processing (Fig. 1c) including cropping, resizing, adding noises, data augmentation, and applying the dynamic image summarization method. The aim of cropping is delimiting the cow area by eliminating noisy pixels coming from sunlight or any noisy effects. Next, these cropped images were resized to 224×224 pixels (Fig. 2a) for the network training process. To ensure a good performance of the CNN model and test its stability, we added some noisy effects on images by randomly changing the brightness of images. In addition, to avoid overfitting issues, we applied the data augmentation technique by lightening the edges of the frames using negative effect (Fig. 2b) and gamma correction effect with 0.5 adjustment parameter (Fig. 2c). These corrections can be made even on low-quality images which can brighten the object threshold and facilitate the learning process. The obtained frames are generated using the dynamic image method. This method is able to summarize video content in single RGB image representation, using the rank pooling method [23] to construct a vector d^* that contains enough information to rank all T frames $I_1, \ldots, I_T$ in the video and make a standard RGB image (Fig. 2d) using the $RankSVM$ [45] formulation:

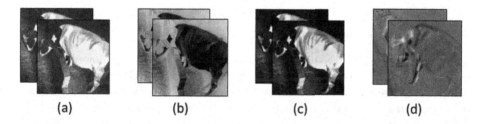

| (a) | (b) | (c) | (d) |

Fig. 2. Example of resultant frames from the pre-processing stage.

$$d^* = p(I_1, \ldots, I_T; \psi) = \arg\min_d E(d)$$

$$E(d) = \frac{\lambda}{2}||d||^2 + \frac{2}{T(T-1)} \sum_{q>t} \max\{0, 1 - S(q|d) + S(t|d)\}. \tag{1}$$

Where $d \in \mathbb{R}^d$ and $\psi(I_t) \in \mathbb{R}^d$ are vectors of parameters and image features, respectively while λ is a regularization parameter. Up to time t, the time average of these features is calculated using $V_t = \frac{1}{t} \sum_{T=1}^{t} \psi(I_T)$. The ranking function associates to each time t a score $S(t|d) = \langle d, V_t \rangle$. The second term is constructed to test how many pairs are correctly ranked: if at least a unit margin is present, then the pair is well ranked, i.e. $S(q|d) > S(t|d) + 1$ with $q > t$.

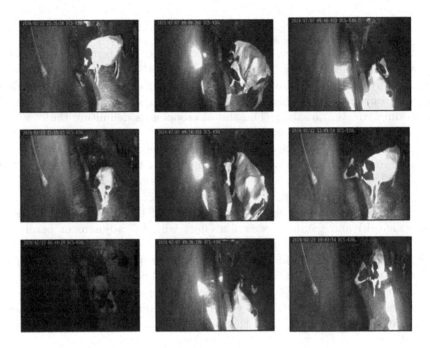

Fig. 3. Sample frames from the collected dataset.

3.3 Dynamic Image Approach

The dynamic image (Fig. 1d) is a CNN-based approach which powerfully recognizes motion and temporal features from a standard RGB image. It uses a compact representation of video that summarizes the motion of moving actors in a single frame. Interestingly, the dynamic image approach uses a standard CNN architecture pre-trained in still image Benchmark. This approach proved [23] its efficiency in learning long-term dynamics and accurately performed 89.1% of accuracy using the CaffeNet model trained on ImageNet and fine-tuned on UCF101 dataset [46].

3.4 Key Architectures

To recognize rumination behavior of dairy cow, we used an end-to-end architecture that can efficiently recognize long-term dynamics and temporal features with a standard CNN architecture as it was presented in Sect. 3.3. To ensure good performance of our system, we chose to use only two well-known key architectures: VGG [47] and ResNet [48,49] that were adopted and tested in Sect. 4. These two models are powerful and useful for image classification tasks. They achieved remarkable performance on ImageNet Benchmark [50] which make them the core of multiple novel CNN-based approaches [51,52]. The VGG model presents two main versions: VGG16 model with 16-layers and VGG19 model with 19-layers. ResNet model presents more than two versions that can handle a large number of layers with a strong performance using the so-called technique "identity shortcut connection" that enables the network to skip one or more layers.

3.5 Overfitting Prevention Method

Overfitting occurs when the model learns noises from the dataset while training, which make the learning performance much better on the training set than on the test set. To prevent these inferences, we adopted few regularization methods to improve the performance of the model. The first technique adopted is the dropout method [53], which can reduce interdependency among neurons by randomly dropping layers and connections during the training phase and thus forcing nodes within a layer to be more active and more adapted to correct mistakes from prior layers. The second technique is the data augmentation method, which prevents the model from overfitting all samples by increasing the diversity of images available for the training phase using different filters such as those presented in Sect. 3.3. The third technique is the early stopping method [54], which tracks and optimize the performance of the model by planting a trigger that stops the training process when the test error starts to increase and the train error starts decrease.

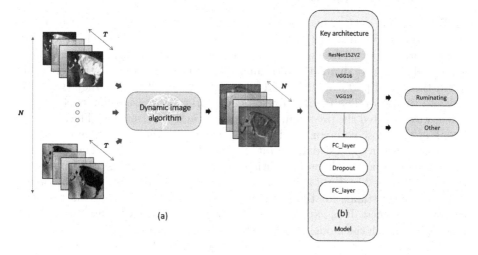

Fig. 4. Cow rumination behavior recognition procedures.

4 Experiments

In this section, we present the implementation process of the proposed model and the adopted evaluation metrics (Sect. 4.1). Subsequently, we evaluate the obtained results of rumination behavior recognition (Sect. 4.2). Finally, we compare the proposed model with other architectures (Sect. 4.3).

4.1   Implementation

We empirically evaluated the cow rumination behavior recognition using cow generated dataset as detailed in Sect. 3.2. For classification tasks, we implemented three pretrained CNN-base models: VGG16, VGG19, and ResNet152V2 to evaluate each model performance on the generated dataset. In the fine-tuning stage, we froze parameters of upper layers and replaced the rest of the layers by other layers as depicted in Fig. 4b. The dropout ratio was set to 0.5 to prevent overfitting. We used Adam optimizer [55] with an intial learning rate $lr_0 = 0.001$ and eventually change its value during the training stage using the exponential decay formula:

$$lr = lr_0 \times e^{kt} \tag{2}$$

Where t and k correspond to the iteration number and the decay steps, respectively. Models were trained on GPUs with batch size = 12.

Let $T = \{25, 50, 100\}$ be the number of frames used to generate a dynamic image (Fig. 4a). The aim is to evaluate the performance of the network with short video sequences. As for the rest of this study, we refer the datasets that contains dynamic images generated from 25, 50, and 100 frames for a single image as T25, T50 and T100, respectively.

4.2   Evaluation Approach

In Table 2, the evaluation stage is made of two trials: in trial 1, we tested the model only on the generated data without data augmentation. In trial 2, we added more generated frames using the data augmentation technique. The whole generated data were divided into training and testing sets. In each trial, we evaluated the model performance based on accuracy, validation accuracy (val_acc), loss and validation loss (val_loss) results as metrics to measure model efficiency. Then, we evaluated the precision, the sensitivity and AUC metrics. The accuracy is one of the most common used metrics that count the percentage of correct classifications for the test data and it is calculated using Eq. (3). The loss value calculates the error of the model during the optimization process. The precision metric is obtained by Eq. (4) is consistent with the percentage of the outcomes. The sensitivity stands for the percentage of the total relevant results that are correctly classified. It is expressed using Eq. (5). The Area Under Curve AUC reflects how much the model is capable to distinguish between classes. The higher the AUC, the better the network is predicting classes. To measure the effectiveness of the model, machine learning uses the confusion matrix which contains four main variable: True Positive (TP), True Negative (TN), False Positive (FP) and False Negative (FN).

$$Accuracy = \frac{TP + TN}{TP + FP + TN + FN} \tag{3}$$

$$Precision = \frac{TP}{TP + FP} \tag{4}$$

$$Sensitivity = \frac{TP}{TP + FN} \tag{5}$$

4.3 Evaluation Results

In the first experiment, the performance of the proposed model was lower in the evaluation phase than in training phase. VGG16 gave important results with 91% of accuracy using T25. However, with the growth of data size the network values did not improve accordingly. On other hand, the performance got higher with both of datasets T50 and T100. There are 5.89%, 7.93% and 6.05% boosts of accuracies with T50 dataset using ResNet152V2, VGG16 and VGG19 models, respectively. In the second experiment, there are remarkable improvements with highest accuracy obtained by VGG16 using T100 dataset. With the presented AUC and loss results in Fig. 5 and accuracy value equal to 98.12%, the network has proven its potential in predicting the rumination behavior. To ensure the reliability and efficiency of the model, we present the sensitivity and precision results in the Table 3 using T100 dataset.

Table 2. Results of cow rumination behavior model.

Trial	N° frames	Key architecture	Dataset size	Loss	Val_loss	Accuracy	Val_acc
1	T = 25	ResNet152V2	N = 1015 Test = 213	0.0359	0.7463	98.73%	84.04%
		VGG-16		0.2081	0.2922	91.34%	90.61%
		VGG-19		0.2874	0.3241	88.17%	88.73%
	T = 50	ResNet152V2	N = 508 Test = 107	0.0207	0.7929	99.86%	82.24%
		VGG-16		0.1697	0.3679	92.39%	85.98%
		VGG-19		0.2453	0.3600	88.45%	86.92%
	T = 100	ResNet152V2	N = 254 Test = 53	0.0050	0.7851	100%	84.91%
		VGG-16		0.1200	0.4572	95.76%	86.79%
		VGG-19		0.1363	0.3805	95.20%	84.91%
2	T = 25	ResNet152V2	N = 2030 Test = 426	0.1153	0.8742	95.46%	81.46%
		VGG-16		0.1370	0.3706	94.19%	90.85%
		VGG-19		0.2186	0.3045	90.78%	88.97%
	T = 50	ResNet152V2	N = 2032 Test = 427	0.0449	0.3687	98.12%	88.13%
		VGG-16		0.0794	0.1944	96.91%	93.91%
		VGG-19		0.1375	0.2108	94.44%	92.97%
	T = 100	ResNet15V2	N = 1016 Test = 213	0.0277	0.3246	98.95%	93.90%
		VGG-16		0.0648	**0.0707**	0.9754	**98.12%**
		VGG-19		0.1049	0.0821	95.01%	97.65%

Both of VGG16 and VGG19 achieved higher than 97% in both precision and recall metrics, which proves the robustness of the network. We notice that VGG16 achieved the best performance by accurately predicting 99% of rumination behavior. To ensure that the model is performing well with different test sets, we conduct 10 folds cross-validation and present the average, Standard Deviation (STD) values of accuracy and AUC metrics. The results of this procedure are detailed in the Fig. 6, knowing that K is the number of folds.

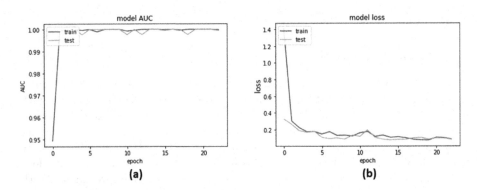

Fig. 5. Results of (a) train AUC, test AUC, (b) train loss and test loss during the training phase using VGG16 key architecture finetuned on T100 dataset with data augmentation.

Table 3. Recall and precision of three models using the T100.

		Recall	Precision	Number of frames
VGG16	Rumination	99%	97%	110
	Other	97%	99%	103
VGG19	Rumination	98%	97%	110
	Other	97%	98%	103
ResNet152V2	Rumination	98%	91%	110
	other	89%	98%	103

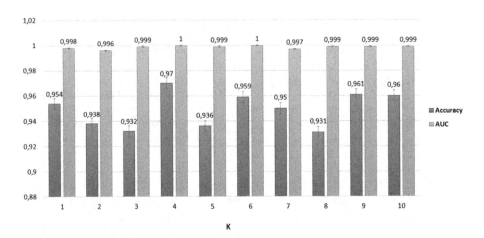

Fig. 6. Average and STD of the accuracy and AUC metrics using 10 fold cross-validation with VGG 16 as the base network.

With these obtained results, the model has proved its potential in predicting and recognizing cow rumination behavior with remarkable highest and lowest average accuracy equal to 93% and 97%, respectively. The STD accuracy of the network varies between 2.7% and 6.9%. In addition, most of average AUC results are close to 1.00 while the AUC std values are less than 1.2%, which demonstrate the efficiency and the reliability of our method in recognizing behavior.

4.4   Comparison

To make the comparison more significant, we compare our proposed method with ResNet50, ResNet152, InceptionV3 [56] and DenseNet121 [57] models using T100 generated dataset. The efficiency of the model is done using the accuracy, mean precision and mean recall metrics. The mean precision and recall were calculated using the obtained results during the training stage. The results of the classification are detailed in Table 4.

Table 4. Comparison of DenseNet121, InceptionV3, ResNet50 and Resnet152 models with VGG16 architecture using T100 dataset.

Key architecture	Accuracy	Mean precision	Mean recall
DenseNet121	93%	93.5%	93.5%
InceptionV3	92%	92%	92%
ResNet50	78%	82%	79%
ResNet152	75%	74.5%	74.5%
VGG16	**98%**	**98%**	**98%**

Overall, VGG16 performs favourably against the other architectures. Compared with the presented results, most of models performed less than 98%. DenseNet121 network achieved 93.5% in both of mean precision and recall metrics. InceptionV3 gave 92% of accuracy, recall and precision results. However, both of ResNet50 and ResNet152 performed less than 82%.

5   Conclusion

In this paper, we proposed an effective recognition method with video to monitor and classify cow behavior using deep learning approaches. These technologies proved their potential in complex environments such as farms. They enabled conducting a monitoring method without appealing to these attached and invasive devices. Despite the surrounding inferences (e.g., sunlight and poor lighting) that produced undesirable effects on cow movements such as chewing or swallowing behaviors, we were able to accurately recognize these deep features of rumination behavior using all postures of the dairy cow. Our network basis is simple and easy-to-use based on a standard CNN-based deep learning models. Through an

RGB image, the network can recognize long-term dynamics using a compacted representation of a video. The proposed method achieved competitive prediction performance with 98.12% of accuracy. Future works include the extension of our monitoring method to track rumination time and cows physical activity such as walking and resting.

Acknowledgment. This research work is supported by LifeEye LLC. The statements made herein are solely the responsibility of the authors.

References

1. Bouwman, A., Van der Hoek, K., Eickhout, B., Soenario, I.: Exploring changes in world ruminant production systems. Agric. Syst. **84**(2), 121–153 (2005)
2. Thomsen, D.K., et al.: Negative thoughts and health: associations among rumination, immunity, and health care utilization in a young and elderly sample. Psychosom. Med. **66**(3), 363–371 (2004)
3. Stangaferro, M., Wijma, R., Caixeta, L., Al-Abri, M., Giordano, J.: Use of rumination and activity monitoring for the identification of dairy cows with health disorders: Part iii. metritis. J. Dairy Sci. **99**(9), 7422–7433 (2016)
4. Vandevala, T., Pavey, L., Chelidoni, O., Chang, N.-F., Creagh-Brown, B., Cox, A.: Psychological rumination and recovery from work in intensive care professionals: associations with stress, burnout, depression and health. J. Intensive Care **5**(1), 16 (2017)
5. Nolen-Hoeksema, S.: The role of rumination in depressive disorders and mixed anxiety/depressive symptoms. J. Abnorm. Psychol. **109**(3), 504 (2000)
6. Grinter, L., Campler, M., Costa, J.: Validation of a behavior-monitoring collar's precision and accuracy to measure rumination, feeding, and resting time of lactating dairy cows. J. Dairy Sci. **102**(4), 3487–3494 (2019)
7. Suzuki, T., et al.: Effect of fiber content of roughage on energy cost of eating and rumination in Holstein cows. Anim. Feed Sci. Technol. **196**, 42–49 (2014)
8. Beauchemin, K.A.: Ingestion and mastication of feed by dairy cattle. Vet. Clin. N. Am. Food Anim. Pract. **7**(2), 439–463 (1991)
9. Reith, S., Brandt, H., Hoy, S.: Simultaneous analysis of activity and rumination time, based on collar-mounted sensor technology, of dairy cows over the peri-estrus period. Livestock Sci. **170**, 219–227 (2014)
10. Paudyal, S., Maunsell, F., Richeson, J., Risco, C., Donovan, A., Pinedo, P.: Peripartal rumination dynamics and health status in cows calving in hot and cool seasons. J. Dairy Sci. **99**(11), 9057–9068 (2016)
11. Calamari, L., Soriani, N., Panella, G., Petrera, F., Minuti, A., Trevisi, E.: Rumination time around calving: an early signal to detect cows at greater risk of disease. J. Dairy Sci. **97**(6), 3635–3647 (2014)
12. Krause, M., Beauchemin, K., Rode, L., Farr, B., Nørgaard, P.: Fibrolytic enzyme treatment of barley grain and source of forage in high-grain diets fed to growing cattle. J. Anim. Sci. **76**(11), 2912–2920 (1998)
13. Lopreiato, V., et al.: Post-weaning rumen fermentation of Simmental calves in response to weaning age and relationship with rumination time measured by the Hr-tag rumination-monitoring system. Livestock Sci. **232**, 103918 (2020)
14. Shen, W., Zhang, A., Zhang, Y., Wei, X., Sun, J.: Rumination recognition method of dairy cows based on the change of noseband pressure. Inf. Process. Agric. 2214–3173 (2020). https://doi.org/10.1016/j.inpa.2020.01.005

15. Mao, Y., He, D., Song, H.: Automatic detection of ruminant cows' mouth area during rumination based on machine vision and video analysis technology. Int. J. Agric. Biol. Eng. **12**(1), 186–191 (2019)
16. Shen, W., Cheng, F., Zhang, Y., Wei, X., Fu, Q., Zhang, Y.: Automatic recognition of ingestive-related behaviors of dairy cows based on triaxial acceleration. Inf. Process. Agric. **7**, 427–443 (2020)
17. Jabbar, R., Shinoy, M., Kharbeche, M., Al-Khalifa, K., Krichen, M., Barkaoui, K.: Driver drowsiness detection model using convolutional neural networks techniques for android application. In: 2020 IEEE International Conference on Informatics, IoT, and Enabling Technologies (ICIoT), pp. 237–242. IEEE (2020)
18. Alhazbi, S., Said, A.B., Al-Maadid, A.: Using deep learning to predict stock movements direction in emerging markets: the case of Qatar stock exchange. In: 2020 IEEE International Conference on Informatics, IoT, and Enabling Technologies (ICIoT), pp. 440–444. IEEE (2020)
19. Said, A.B., Mohamed, A., Elfouly, T., Abualsaud, K., Harras, K.: Deeplearning and low rank dictionary model for mHealth data classification. In: 2018 14th International Wireless Communications & Mobile Computing Conference (IWCMC), pp. 358–363. IEEE (2018)
20. Abdelhedi, M., et al.: Prediction of uniaxial compressive strength of carbonate rocks and cement mortar using artificial neural network and multiple linear regressions. Acta Geodynamica et Geromaterialia **17**(3), 367–378 (2020)
21. Chen, Y., Li, W., Sakaridis, C., Dai, D., Van Gool, L.: Domain adaptive faster R-CNN for object detection in the wild. In: Proceedings of the IEEE Conference on Computer Vision and Pattern Recognition, pp. 3339–3348 (2018)
22. Zhang, H., Liu, D., Xiong, Z.: Two-stream action recognition-oriented video super-resolution. In: Proceedings of the IEEE International Conference on Computer Vision, pp. 8799–8808 (2019)
23. Bilen, H., Fernando, B., Gavves, E., Vedaldi, A., Gould, S.: Dynamic image networks for action recognition. In: Proceedings of the IEEE Conference on Computer Vision and Pattern Recognition, pp. 3034–3042 (2016)   .
24. Milone, D.H., Galli, J.R., Cangiano, C.A., Rufiner, H.L., Laca, E.A.: Automatic recognition of ingestive sounds of cattle based on hidden Markov models. Comput. Electron. Agric. **87**, 51–55 (2012)
25. Chelotti, J.O., Vanrell, S.R., Galli, J.R., Giovanini, L.L., Rufiner, H.L.: A pattern recognition approach for detecting and classifying jaw movements in grazing cattle. Comput. Electron. Agric. **145**, 83–91 (2018)
26. Clapham, W.M., Fedders, J.M., Beeman, K., Neel, J.P.: Acoustic monitoring system to quantify ingestive behavior of free-grazing cattle. Comput. Electron. Agric. **76**(1), 96–104 (2011)
27. Chelotti, J.O., et al.: An online method for estimating grazing and rumination bouts using acoustic signals in grazing cattle. Comput. Electron. Agric. **173**, 105443 (2020)
28. Rau, L.M., Chelotti, J.O., Vanrell, S.R., Giovanini, L.L.: Developments on real-time monitoring of grazing cattle feeding behavior using sound. In: 2020 IEEE International Conference on Industrial Technology (ICIT), pp. 771–776. IEEE (2020)
29. Zehner, N., Umstätter, C., Niederhauser, J.J., Schick, M.: System specification and validation of a noseband pressure sensor for measurement of ruminating and eating behavior in stable-fed cows. Comput. Electron. Agric. **136**, 31–41 (2017)

30. Martiskainen, P., Järvinen, M., Skön, J.-P., Tiirikainen, J., Kolehmainen, M., Mononen, J.: Cow behaviour pattern recognition using a three-dimensional accelerometer and support vector machines. Appl. Anim. Behav. Sci. **119**(1–2), 32–38 (2009)
31. Rayas-Amor, A.A., et al.: Triaxial accelerometers for recording grazing and ruminating time in dairy cows: an alternative to visual observations. J. Vet. Behav. **20**, 102–108 (2017)
32. Hamilton, A.W., et al.: Identification of the rumination in cattle using support vector machines with motion-sensitive bolus sensors. Sensors **19**(5), 1165 (2019)
33. Li, T., Jiang, B., Wu, D., Yin, X., Song, H.: Tracking multiple target cows' ruminant mouth areas using optical flow and inter-frame difference methods. IEEE Access **7**, 185520–185531 (2019)
34. Cheng, Y.: Mean shift, mode seeking, and clustering. IEEE Trans. Pattern Anal. Mach. Intell. **17**(8), 790–799 (1995)
35. Zhang, K., Zhang, L., Liu, Q., Zhang, D., Yang, M.-H.: Fast visual tracking via dense spatio-temporal context learning. In: Fleet, D., Pajdla, T., Schiele, B., Tuytelaars, T. (eds.) ECCV 2014. LNCS, vol. 8693, pp. 127–141. Springer, Cham (2014). https://doi.org/10.1007/978-3-319-10602-1_9
36. Yujuan, C., Dongjian, H., Yinxi, F., Huaibo, S.: Intelligent monitoring method of cow ruminant behavior based on video analysis technology. Int. J. Agric. Biol. Eng. **10**(5), 194–202 (2017)
37. Chen, Y., He, D., Song, H.: Automatic monitoring method of cow ruminant behavior based on spatio-temporal context learning. Int. J. Agric. Biol. Eng. **11**(4), 179–185 (2018)
38. Achour, B., Belkadi, M., Filali, I., Laghrouche, M., Lahdir, M.: Image analysis for individual identification and feeding behaviour monitoring of dairy cows based on convolutional neural networks (cnn). Biosyst. Eng. **198**, 31–49 (2020)
39. Li, D., Chen, Y., Zhang, K., Li, Z.: Mounting behaviour recognition for pigs based on deep learning. Sensors **19**(22), 4924 (2019)
40. Huang, G.-B., Zhu, Q.-Y., Siew, C.-K.: Extreme learning machine: a new learning scheme of feedforward neural networks. In: 2004 IEEE International Joint Conference on Neural Networks (IEEE Cat. No. 04CH37541), vol. 2, pp. 985–990. IEEE (2004)
41. Yang, Q., Xiao, D., Lin, S.: Feeding behavior recognition for group-housed pigs with the faster R-CNN. Comput. Electron. Agric. **155**, 453–460 (2018)
42. Ren, S., He, K., Girshick, R., Sun, J.: Faster R-CNN: towards real-time object detection with region proposal networks. In: Advances in Neural Information Processing Systems, pp. 91–99 (2015)
43. Ambriz-Vilchis, V., Jessop, N., Fawcett, R., Shaw, D., Macrae, A.: Comparison of rumination activity measured using rumination collars against direct visual observations and analysis of video recordings of dairy cows in commercial farm environments. J. Dairy Sci. **98**(3), 1750–1758 (2015)
44. Fenner, K., Yoon, S., White, P., Starling, M., McGreevy, P.: The effect of noseband tightening on horses' behavior, eye temperature, and cardiac responses. PLoS ONE **11**(5), e0154179 (2016)
45. Smola, A.J., Schölkopf, B.: A tutorial on support vector regression. Stat. Comput. **14**(3), 199–222 (2004)
46. Soomro, K., Zamir, A.R., Shah, M.: UCF101: a dataset of 101 human actions classes from videos in the wild. arXiv preprint arXiv:1212.0402 (2012)
47. Simonyan, K., Zisserman, A.: Very deep convolutional networks for large-scale image recognition. arXiv preprint arXiv:1409.1556 (2014)

48. He, K., Zhang, X., Ren, S., Sun, J.: Deep residual learning for image recognition. In: Proceedings of the IEEE Conference on Computer Vision and Pattern Recognition, pp. 770–778 (2016)
49. He, K., Zhang, X., Ren, S., Sun, J.: Identity mappings in deep residual networks. In: Leibe, B., Matas, J., Sebe, N., Welling, M. (eds.) ECCV 2016. LNCS, vol. 9908, pp. 630–645. Springer, Cham (2016). https://doi.org/10.1007/978-3-319-46493-0_38
50. Krizhevsky, A., Sutskever, I., Hinton, G.E.: ImageNet classification with deep convolutional neural networks. In: Advances in Neural Information Processing Systems, pp. 1097–1105 (2012)
51. Donahue, J., et al.: Long-term recurrent convolutional networks for visual recognition and description. In: Proceedings of the IEEE Conference on Computer Vision and Pattern Recognition, pp. 2625–2634 (2015). https://doi.org/10.1109/CVPR.2015.7298878
52. Wu, Z., Pan, S., Chen, F., Long, G., Zhang, C., Philip, S.Y.: A comprehensive survey on graph neural networks. IEEE Trans. Neural Netw. Learn. Syst. (2020)
53. Srivastava, N., Hinton, G., Krizhevsky, A., Sutskever, I., Salakhutdinov, R.: Dropout: a simple way to prevent neural networks from overfitting. J. Mach. Learn. Res. 15(1), 1929–1958 (2014)
54. Prechelt, L.: Early stopping - but when? In: Orr, G.B., Müller, K.-R. (eds.) Neural Networks: Tricks of the Trade. LNCS, vol. 1524, pp. 55–69. Springer, Heidelberg (1998). https://doi.org/10.1007/3-540-49430-8_3
55. Kingma, D.P., Ba, J.: Adam: a method for stochastic optimization. arXiv preprint arXiv:1412.6980 (2014)
56. Szegedy, C., Vanhoucke, V., Ioffe, S., Shlens, J., Wojna, Z.: Rethinking the inception architecture for computer vision. In: Proceedings of the IEEE Conference on Computer Vision and Pattern Recognition, pp. 2818–2826 (2016)
57. Huang, G., Liu, Z., Van Der Maaten, L., Weinberger, K.Q.: Densely connected convolutional networks. In: Proceedings of the IEEE Conference on Computer Vision and Pattern Recognition, pp. 4700–4708 (2017)

EAP-NOOB-KRB for Mutual Authentication in IoT Environment

Wala Kharouf[1(✉)] and Mohamed Abid[2]

[1] Laboratory Hatem Bettaher Irescomtah, Faculty of Science of Gabes, University of Gabes, Gabes, Tunisia
kharoufwala24@gmail.com

[2] Laboratory Hatem Bettaher Irescomtah, National School of Engineering of Gabes, University of Gabes, Gabes, Tunisia
mohamed.abid@enig.rnu.tn

Abstract. The *Internet of Things (IoT)* is the driver of security and system control science and creativity for the elderly. Another protection challenge that needs to be addressed is the *bootstraping*. The newly installed computer completes a series of operations during the startup process so that it can access the network as a dependent member. One of the methods currently offered by the *IETF EAP Method Update (EMU) Working Group (WG)* is the use of the *Extensible Authentication Protocol (EAP)* to enforce the validation mechanism of *IoT* devices in a more efficient and scalable way. The *EAP-Nimble out-of-band (EAP-NOOB)* operates without pre-configuration and allows for security to be improved by out-of-band networks. in this paper we explain the process of combining the *EAP-NOOB* method with the third-party authentication scheme of *Kerberos* to provide *mutual authentication* in the *IoT* environment. Compared with other methods, the advantage of this method is that it does not require any modification to the access point, so it is easy to deploy at a reasonable cost. Provide security analysis to highlight the robustness of the proposed new protocol.

Keywords: EAP-NOOB · Bootstrapping · IoT · Kerberos · EAP-Kerberos · Mutual authentication

1 Introduction

The security of the *Internet of Things (IoT)* [17] is the focus of ongoing research and development assessments by research agencies, suppliers, and standard organizations. *Bootstraping* is the method of allowing new *IoT* devices to securely access a deployed and running network, among different *IoT* protection methods. In this context, a traditional method of *bootstrapping* [16] is to provide engineering with personalized descriptions that open the door to the development of inter-operable solutions, irrespective of the technology used in the *Internet of Things*. Also, researchers used *Extensible Authentication Protocol (EAP)* [1] in *IoT* environment to run different authentication methods and also to

© Springer Nature Switzerland AG 2020
I. Jemili and M. Mosbah (Eds.): DiCES-N 2020, CCIS 1348, pp. 140–150, 2020.
https://doi.org/10.1007/978-3-030-65810-6_8

exploit the strength of the *AAA (Authentication, Authorisation and accounting)* infrastructure [2,11]. Many works aimed to provide lightweight EAP methods to be deployed in *ISO* lower layers. The first is the *EAP-Nimble out-of-band (EAP-NOOB)* [3] approach authentication and the key derivation is intended for *bootstrapping* all kinds of *Internet of Things (IoT)* devices that have no pre-configured authentication credentials. The second is the *EAP-Kerberos* validation method [9], which allows *IoT* devices to use *Kerberos* credentials to achieve *mutual authentication* with the primary authentication server. The proposed solution called *EAP-NOOB-KRB* aims to combine these two methods to improve *mutual authentication* between *IoT* devices [17].

Another critical requirement for *IoT* devices, is their energy dependence. We need to provide solution that help change connecting devices after each period (for example every 8 h) so that we can have continuous secure connection between devices and servers. That why we want to integrate *Kerberos* in our solution so we can afford ticket with a limited validity duration for each *IoT* device in the access network. *EAP-NOOB-KRB* will take into consideration this requirement.

The reminder of this paper is as follows: The second section provides background information about *EAP-NOOB*, *Kerberos* and *EAP-Kerberos*. In the third section, an overview of the proposed *EAP-NOOB-KRB* is provided. The fourth section is dedicated to the security analysis of the new solution, and finally, we conclude the paper and present some future work.

2 Background and Technical Overview

After the *IoT* device is deployed and started, to get a reliant party on the network and thereby becoming part of the security domain, it must go through a *bootstrapping* method. The startup process entails security protocols such as authentication, authorization, and key management being executed. For operators who need to manage a large number of *IoT* devices in an *IoT* environment, this process is critical. To facilitate separate solutions for every *IoT* technology [17], the *bootstraping* must make sure that it is lightweight, based on common protocols and interoperable. The reminder in this section is as follows: We will discuss *EAP-NOOB* first, then *Kerberos*, and finally *EAP-Kerberos*.

2.1 EAP-NOOB Method

By providing solutions for all types of devices, the widespread use of EAP in bootloaders makes it an interesting research case, especially for *IoT*. *EAP-NOOB* [3] has fascinating properties among all the EAP methods that make it an acceptable solution for the *Internet of Things* [18]. Network registration using *EAP-NOOB* allows devices or EAP peers to establish security associations without authentication. Some pre-configured information is not needed for the system. We will not pre-establish any Identification or security ID in terms of protection. Therefore, the device does not rely on each manufacturer or third party. Also, this method uses the Elliptic Curve Diffie-Hellman (ECDH) key agreement protocol to exchange a shared key between the peer and the server. A special function of *EAP-NOOB* is that it includes channels that are out-of-band (OOB) to guarantee that protected data is not transmitted via a single channel. The third function supported route sends a random number from the peer to the server named (Noob) and an fingerprint (Hoob), and vice versa. The restricted computer must have at least one input or output interface (e.g., camera, display, re-alarm LED) to perform this operation. *EAP-NOOB* is divided into several stages, and an EAP conversion is per level. There are some EAP conversations therefore:

Initial Exchange: Launch a handshake phase to discuss parameters for configuration. For present and future EAP communications, the client and the server share peer IDs. They swap random numbers and create a mutual key using ECDH exchange. This EAP conversation intentionally ends with *EAP-Failure*. This step cannot guarantee *mutual authentication* between the two peers because it ends with an *EAP-Failure*. Therefore, we have a shared key, but the authentication is weak.

Waiting Exchange: The third party usually the user must complete the OOB phase after forming an association between the client and the server. The process waits for a certain time and then attempts to link to the server using *EAP-NOOB*. If the out-of-band operation is ended, it will restart at the end of the exchange. Otherwise the dialog concludes with *EAP-Failure*, and the system can replay the interaction after the time is over.

Completion Exchange: At this point, the two entities exchange message verification codes to verify whether the shared frozen recording materials are reliable. Therefore, the conversation concludes with *EAP-success* if the information is accurate, and the two machines will retain a persistent *EAP-NOOB* association.

In addition, it performs fast re-connection exchanges to avoid repeating OOB steps [3], and allows the device to reconnect using previously associated encryption hardware.

2.2   Kerberos Authentication Protocol

Kerberos [4] is a commonly used authentication method. In *Kerberos*, the authentication method requires the principal and the *Key Distribution Center (KDC)*. The topic represents users and facilities registered in the realm of *Kerberos*. A master database is managed by *KDC* and a key is allocated to each subject. Each client must submit valid *Kerberos* credentials to ensure access to the service. Next, we introduce *Kerberos* credentials and explain how to get and employ them to authenticate service users.

2.2.1   Kerberos Credentials

The client must submit a credential consisting of two components, a ticket and an authenticator, to access a specific service. A ticket is a message that was created and encrypted by *KDC* with the private key of the requesting service.

It includes client authentication information and a secret session key. Using the private key exchanged with the *KDC*, when the service accepts a ticket, it may decode it and retrieve the secret session key. The customer must ensure that they have the same passkey to verify their identity with the supplier. This is achieved using an authenticator that holds the client information which must be encrypted with a hidden session key. If the authenticator has been successfully decrypted using the hidden session key received from the ticket, offer the service to the customer.

2.2.2   Kerberos Exchange

The *Kerberos* protocol specifies three exchanges, namely:

- *Authentication Server (AS)* exchange.
- *Ticket Granting Service (TGS)* exchange.
- Client server *(Application AP)* exchange.

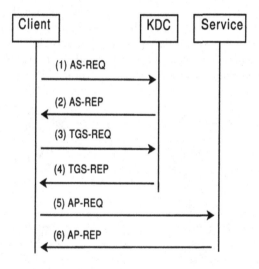

Fig. 1. The Kerberos authentication exchange.

These three exchanges are seen in (Fig. 1). The interchange of the AS makes client to obtain the credentials which it can use to prove its identity to the TGS. These vouchers include a ticket called a *Ticket Granting Ticket (TGT)* and an appeal meeting TGS related to the meeting.

The client initiates with an AS request (AS-REQ) and the AS replies with a message (AS-REP) containing TGT and session key client secrets. After that, the client sends TGS-REQ containing TGT and the authenticator. Then, TGS replies by sending a (TGS-REP) containing new service Ticket and another shared secret between the client and the service.

After the client gets the session key, the AP (AP-REQ) can perform identity verification based on the service ticket and the authenticator (identity verification). Finally, the AP send an acknowledgment message (AP-REP) so client can start using the service.

2.3 EAP-Kerberos Authentication Method

2.3.1 Overview

The verification mechanism proposed in [5] explains in detail how to the and the existing RADIUS server to the protocol to authenticate the MNs. The network access control architecture relies on the *Kerberos* authentication protocol ticket caching mechanism to improve transmission performance under roaming conditions.

Traditionally, in a roaming situation, when the mobile node MN is near a new access point, it will disassociate from the old AP and join the new AP. Contact the MN's home RADIUS server [12] to perform *mutual authentication* between the MN and the new AP. The cross-domain exchanging of messages between the RADIUS node on the network visited and the RADIUS server on the home network will cause a delay in transmission, resulting in the loss of packets and the reduction of service quality [6]. The *EAP-Kerberos* method [9] decreases the transfer time by avoiding the need to access the home network server while transmission is carried out by a roaming MN.

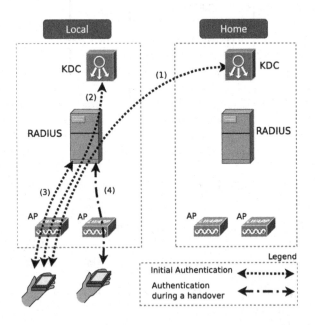

Fig. 2. Overview of EAP-Kerberos authentication in a roaming scenario.

As shown in the (Fig. 2), in order to use *EAP-Kerberos* to authenticate the roaming station (Mobile Node MN) [10], the latter first gets the authentication information (TGT) from its local KDC. *Kerberos* messages can be relayed between the MN and the local (visited) KDC by the AP and RADIUS server of the visited network (1). In order to receive a service fare, the MN swaps the TGT received from the original KDC with the visited TGS (2). Network-accessing APs and RADIUS servers also relay this interaction. The MN then uses the service ticket in the AP switch to perform *mutual authentication* with the RADIUS server of the visited network (3).

The same service ticket received in the initial authentication process will be used in the AP exchange when the MN needs to connect with a new AP to authenticate the MN via the RADIUS server of the access network visited (4). Since the MN will re-authenticate in the same visited the network, compared with the initial validation, the re-authentication exchange is much less affected by network delays and packet loss.

The *EAP-Kerberos* approach allows the MN to make its local network have a *Kerberos* username name and password pair. If an inter-domain agreement exists between the local network of the MN and the network visited, the MN can use its *Kerberos* login name and password to execute *EAP-Kerberos* authentication on the network visited. The *EAP-Kerberos* technique often includes nearly coordinated timepieces for all organizations involved in authentication (EAP peers, servers, and KDCs). The clock almost set is configurable in most *Kerberos* implementations, usually around 5 min. The explanation for this restriction is that for detecting repeat communications, the *Kerberos* server uses technology based on poorly synchronized clocks, replay buffers, and time stamps.

3   EAP-NOOB-KRB Authentication Method

The *EAP-NOOB-KRB* authentication method allows clients on the network to use *Kerberos* credentials to perform mutual validation with the primary authentication server in the wireless access network. The proposed method requires each network provider to employ one or more KDC deployed in the *Kerberos* realm, and the network client must be registered in the *Kerberos* master database. To access the network, the MN must have a *Kerberos* login name and password pair, which can be used to authenticate the network provider's KDC. Since the intial exchange of *EAP-NOOB* don't guarantee *mutual authentication* between the two peers, *EAP-NOOB-KRB* will integrate *Kerberos* authentication echanges to provide *mutual authentication*. In the following subsections, we introduce the new solution operations and detail the steps of the *EAP-NOOB-KRB* authentication method. We discuss also the *EAP-NOOB-KRB* re-authentication mechanism.

3.1   Overview

The method we propose is based on the concept of network access area. We define the network access zone as a collection of lightweight access points managed by a single back-end authentication server. A group of network access areas belonging to the same provider constitute an access network. Although a medium-sized access network may consist of a single network access range, dividing the access network into different areas is important for larger access networks (for example, the access network of a service provider wireless online). Generally, using multiple regions in a large access network can simplify management and ensure a scalable infrastructure. Assume that for each network access area, there is a KDC managed by the access network provider. In addition, the authentication server that manages a specific zone has the *Kerberos* secret key of the corresponding zone.

Our solution has the same exchanges as for *EAP-NOOB* (i.e Initial, Waiting and Completion). The idea is to profit from the strength of *Kerberos* authentication protocol to enhance the Initial exchange of *EAP-NOOB*. We called our proposed solution *EAP-NOOB-KRB*. The authentication server is allowed to verify the *Kerberos* AS-REQ message received from wireless clients requesting access to the area through the initial exchange of *EAP-NOOB*. The MN must acquire a service ticket for the LAN access area in order to secure network access in the field, and provide the ticket to the authentication server in the zone. The *EAP-NOOB-KRB* approach mentioned below is how the MN acquires and uses *Kerberos* credentials to authenticate and obtain the network.

3.2   EAP-NOOB-KRB Operations

The Negotiation between the peer and the authentication server in *EAP-NOOB-KRB* method shown in (Fig. 3) is similar to the *EAP-NOOB* method [3] and organized as follow:

1. The initial exchange includes a joint handshake. The first EAP-NOOB-KRB request (Type = 2) submitted by the authentication server includes the name of the *Kerberos* realm and the information identifying the access zone to the local network, the PeerId of the peer, the version (version) of the protocol, and the cipher suite (Cryptosuites). It supports OOB channel direction indicators (Dirs) and ServerInfo objects.
2. After receiving the first message, the server will check whether there is a *Kerberos* service ticket for the local area in its credential cache. If there is such a ticket, the peer sends the *EAP-NOOB-KRB response* (Type = 2) Response. The OOB channel direction selected by the peer (Dirp) and PeerInfo object.
3. Server relies the AS-REQ to the KDC.
4. The KDC replies with AS-REP.
5. Server sends *EAP-NOOB-KRB request* (Type = 3) along with the public components of its ECDHE key and nonce Ns, PKs, and added TGT from the AS.
6. Then, the peer sends an *EAP-NOOB-KRB request* (type = 3) response to him, which is part of the server's ECDHE key and random number (PKp, Np, domain = domain.Com, TGS-REQ).

7. Server relies the TGS-REQ to the KDC containing the TGT.
8. KDC replies with TGS-REP containing the Service Ticket TS.
9. The TGS-REP response message from KDC is returned to the slave in the *EAP-NOOB-KRB request.*
10. The initial exchange of *EAP-NOOB-KRB* always ends with *EAP-Failure* server because the authentication has not yet been completed. The server and the peer join the waiting state OOB(1) in the *EAP-NOOB* process at the completion of the initial exchange [3].

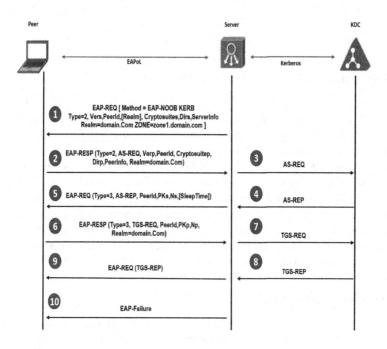

Fig. 3. Initial exchange EAP-NOO-KRB authentication in the home access network.

As a reminder, our solution is based on *EAP-NOOB* and maintains the same exchanges (waiting and completion). The main enhancement of our work concerns the Initial exchange (authentication stage).

3.3 EAP-NOOB-KRB Re-authentication

Compared with existing solutions to reduce EAP re-authentication time (such as *EAP Reauthentication Protocol (ERP)* [14] and IEEE 802.11r [15]), *EAP-NOOB-KBR* can provide a fast re-authentication mechanism, such as *EAP-Kerberos* has three main advantages; (1) The proposed method extends the EAP layer by specifying a new EAP method to ensure that the proposed method has nothing to do with the link layer. (2) The proposed approach does not need to change the access point, so it has advantages from the perspective of deployment cost. (3) *EAP-NOOB-KBR* supports the use of *Kerberos* inter-domain authentication to get the access point and the Internet. We point out that other existing methods only allow quick reconnection within the same access network.

4   Security Analysis

As a security protocol, *EAP-NOOB-KRB* must ensure many safety goals to prevent malicious users from illegally using the infrastructure. Security specifications have been defined by the *IETF* [7], and any new EAP methods designed for wireless LAN and *IoT* must meet these safety requirements. We explain below how the *EAP-NOOB-KRB* solution satisfies these criteria.

4.1   Generation of Symmetric Key Material

AP interchange between MN and the home is used in the *EAP-NOOB-KRB* technique database for access authentication. Normally, when using ECDH, EAP Server and MN will exchange another shared secret key but with lack of authentication. Therefore, using *Kerberos* will prove the identity of the two peer and provide *mutual authentication*. Then, MNs and servers use the shared secret key to derive other key material. The *EAP-NOOB-KRB* method uses AP exchange between the MN and the home access authentication server. Normally, when ECDH is employed, EAP Server and MN will exchange another shared key, but lack of authentication. Therefore, using *Kerberos* will prove the identity of two peers and provide *mutual authentication*. Then, the MNs and the servers use the shared key to derive other key materials.

4.2   Mutual Authentication

As mentioned earlier, *EAP-NOOB* when using ECDH has a major disadvantage, namely the lack of an authentication mechanism. Using *Kerberos*, an AP exchange is done by the MN and the authentication server, and the server will authenticate the MN by checking the authenticator received in the AP-REQ message. MN verify, on the other hand, is the authentication server's identity after checking the AP-REP post. On the other hand, the MN verifies the identity of the authentication server after verifying the AP-REP message. The *EAP-NOOB-KRB* method requires peers to request *mutual authentication* in the AP-REQ message by setting mutually necessary options.

4.3   Preventing Replay Attacks

In order to detect replayed messages, *EAP-NOOB-KRB* inherits the *Kerberos* replay buffer, in which the messages are stored for a predetermined time. If the received message is not the most recent message (the timestamp contained is too old.) or is the same as the message in the "replay cache", the message is considered to be repeated and discarded.

4.4   Preventing Man-In-The-Middle Attacks

Sensitive information in *Kerberos* exchanges is protected by encryption mechanisms that include integrity protection. The unencrypted part of the message uses an encrypted checksum for integrity protection. Moreover, as the EAP peer identity is enclosed in the ticket and the server's identity is found in the TGS-REP packet, the *Kerberos* protocol provides cryptographic linking. Therefore, both parties clearly know the identity of the EAP peer and the server. Finally, integrity protection, prevention of replay, binding of password and independence of session is specified in [8]. All mechanisms of defense against attacks by the man-in-the-middle are enforced by the *EAP-NOOB-KRB* system.

5   Conclusion

Due to the proliferation of constrained devices in the *Internet of Things*, existing boot procedures must be adjusted to allow new *IoT* devices to safely connect to existing and running networks. To this end, we can study lightweight stand-alone solutions suitable for any *IoT* technology.

In this article, we design a new approach called *EAP-NOOB-KRB*, which achieves *mutual authentication* between mobile nodes and servers while ensuring acceptable delays. We also show that the *EAP-NOOB-KRB* method meets the security requirements of the *IETF*.

In future work, we can explore new technologies to reduce the message size by integrating the low-overhead CoAP-EAP (LO-CoAP-EAP) process [13]. In addition, to check our assertions and test how various timers affect the entire mechanism of authentication, including *EAP-NOOB* and Waiting Exchange timers, we will conduct real experiments. Furthermore, by expanding the open source hostapd [19] RADIUS server and WPA [20] EAP supplicant, we can introduce the *EAP-NOOB-KRB* process.

References

1. Winter, S., Salowey, J.: Update to the Extensible Authentication Protocol (EAP) Applicability Statement for Application Bridging for Federated Access Beyond Web (ABFAB), RFC 7057, December 2013. https://www.rfc-editor.org/rfc/rfc7057
2. Gross, G., de Laat, C., Spence, D., Gommans, L.H., Vollbrecht, J.: Generic AAA Architecture, RFC 2903, August 2000. https://rfc-editor.org/rfc/rfc2903.txt
3. Aura, T., Sethi, M.: Nimble out-of-band authentication for EAP (EAP-NOOB), Internet Engineering Task Force Internet-Draft draft-aura-eap-noob-08 (2020)
4. Neuman, C., Yu, T., Hartman, S., Raeburn, K.: The Kerberos network authentication service (V5), RFC 4120 (Proposed Standard), July 2005. http://www.ietf.org/rfc/rfc4119.txt
5. Amendment to IEEE Std 802.11. wireless LAN medium access control (MAC) and physical layer (PHY) specifications - Amendment 6: Medium access control (MAC) security enhancements, IEEE Standards (2004)

6. Pawlowski, M.P., Jara, A.J., Ogorzalek, M.J.: EAP for IoT: more efficient transport of authentication data - TEPANOM case study. In: 2015 IEEE 29th International Conference on Advanced Information Networking and Applications Workshops (2015)

7. Garcia-Carrillo, D., Marin-Lopez, R.: Multihop bootstrapping with EAP through CoAP intermediaries for IoT. IEEE Internet Things J. **5**, 4003–4017 (2018)

8. Arifin, A.S., Suryanegara, M., Firdaus, T.S., Asvial, M.: IoT-based maritime application: an experiment of ship radius detection (2017). https://doi.org/10.1145/3175684.3175729

9. Zrelli, S., Shinoda, Y.: EAP-Kerberos: leveraging the Kerberos credential caching mechanism for faster re-authentications in wireless access networks. Center for Information Science Japan Advanced Institute of Science and Technology Ishikawa, Japan (2016)

10. Pawlowski, M.P., Jara, A.J., Ogorzalek, M.J.: Compact extensible authentication protocol for the Internet of Things: enabling scalable and efficient security commissioning (2015)

11. Kolluru, K.K., Paniagua, C., van Deventer, J., Eliasson, J., Delsing, J., DeLong, R.J.: An AAA solution for securing industrial IoT devices using next generation access control (2018)

12. DeKok, A., Lior, A.: Remote Authentication Dial In User Service (RADIUS) Protocol Extensions, RFC 6929, April 2013. https://doi.org/10.17487/RFC6929

13. Garcia-Carrillo, D., Marin-Lopez, R., Kandasamy, A., Pelov, A.: A CoAP-based network access authentication service for low-power wide area networks: LO-CoAP-EAP. Sensors 17(11), 2646 (2017). http://www.mdpi.com/1424-8220/17/11/2646

14. Cao, Z., He, B., Shi, Y., Wu, Q., Zorn, G.: EAP Extensions for the EAP Re-authentication Protocol (ERP), RFC 6696 (Proposed Standard), July 2012. https://datatracker.ietf.org/doc/rfc6696/

15. 802.11r: IEEE Standard for Information technology, Telecommunications and information exchange between systems, Local and metropolitan area networks - Specific requirements Part 11: Wireless LAN Medium Access Control (MAC) and Physical Layer (PHY) Specifications Amendment 2: Fast Basic Service Set (BSS) Transition, IEEE Standards (2008). http://dx.doi.org/10.1109

16. Pritikin, M., Richardson, M., Behringer, M., Bjarnason, S., Watsen, K.: Bootstrapping Remote Secure Key Infrastructures (BRSKI), Internet-Draft draft-ietf-anima-bootstrapping-keyinfra-16, June 2018

17. Dwivedi, A.D., et al.: A decentralized privacy-preserving healthcare blockchain for IoT. Sensors **19**(2), 326 (2019)

18. Malina, L., et al.: A secure publish/subscribe protocol for internet of things. In: Proceedings of the 14th International Conference on Availability, Reliability and Security, pp. 1–10, 26 August 2019

19. hostapd: IEEE 802.11 AP, IEEE 802.1X/WPA/WPA2/EAP/RADIUS Authenticator, July 2010. http://hostap.epitest.fi/hostapd/

20. Linux WPA/WPA2/IEEE 802.1X Supplicant, July 2010. http://hostap.epitest.fi/wpasupplicant

Author Index

Printed in the United States
By Bookmasters